Cybermedicine

Warner V. Slack, M.D.

Cartoons by Charles Slack

Cybermedicine

How Computing Empowers Doctors and Patients for Better Health Care

Foreword by Ralph Nader

 Jossey-Bass Publishers
San Francisco

Substantial discounts on bulk quantities of Jossey-Bass books are available to corporations, professional associations, and other organizations. For details and discount information, contact the special sales department at Jossey-Bass Inc., Publishers (415) 433-1740; Fax (800) 605-2665.

For sales outside the United States, please contact your local Simon & Schuster International Office.

Jossey-Bass Web address: http://www.josseybass.com

 Manufactured in the United States of America on Lyons Falls Turin Book. This paper is acid-free and 100 percent totally chlorine-free.

Library of Congress Cataloging-in-Publication Data

Slack, Warner V., [date]
　　Cybermedicine : how computing empowers doctors and patients for better health care / Warner V. Slack. — 1st ed.
　　　　p.　cm.
　　Includes bibliographical references and index.
　　ISBN 0–7879–0343–4 (alk. paper)
　　1. Medical informatics.　2. Physician and patient.　I. Title.
　　[DNLM:　1. Computers.　2. Medical Informatics Applications.
3. Practice Management, Medical.　4. Physician-Patient Relations.
WS 26.55.C7 S631c 1997]
R858.S556　1997
610'.285—dc21
DNLM/DLC
for Library of Congress
　　　　　　　　　　　　　　　　　　　　　　　　　　　　97–3821
　　　　　　　　　　　　　　　　　　　　　　　　　　　　CIP

FIRST EDITION
HB Printing　　　10 9 8 7 6 5 4 3 2 1

—⁓— Contents

For Carolyn

⟞∿⟝ Foreword

Cybermedicine is a book resting on a seeming paradox—a very compassionate, patient-first physician pressing for bolder and more comprehensive computer uses in clinical medicine and in direct patient interaction. Dr. Warner V. Slack, a pioneer in clinical computing (starting in the 1960s at the University of Wisconsin Medical School and later at the Center for Clinical Computing and Harvard Medical School), argues in this work that there is no necessary paradox at all, if the evolution of computers in medicine adheres to what is best for patients and their enhanced role as decision makers.

And what are the guidelines that would enable the computer to have "a humanizing influence on the practice of medicine" and "help patients and their families maintain better health, manage medical problems when they occur, seek and use health care facilities in an enlightened manner, and participate as partners with clinicians in medical decisions that can both improve the quality and reduce the cost of medical care"? There are eight, according to Dr. Slack. Before the programs become widespread, "They should be medically sound; they should be easy to use; they should be truly interactive; they should be of immediate and, if possible, long-range benefit to the patient; they should protect confidentiality; they should be fast and reliable; they should be readily available to people of all socioeconomic backgrounds; and they should be studied for safety and effectiveness."

However comprehensive, these standards do represent a tall order, especially given the stigmas, phobias, and computer illiteracy that impede a clear highway in the minds of many. Especially given those hospital bureaucracies and administrative myopias, which Dr. Slack, putting on his estimable literary scrubs, dissects and parodies mercilessly near the end of the book in a brilliant finale, graced by a poignant description of his young diabetic grandson.

What is so attractive about *Cybermedicine* is that Dr. Slack is no gee-whiz technophile, breathlessly promoting a scenario of inevitable technology for a brave new world of diagnosis, treatment, prevention, and self-help. He permeates his book with continual skepticism in order to discipline his enthusiasm. And well he might, knowing, as he demonstrates, the past failures, overpromises, misuses, and dehumanizations of other technologies, including more than a few of the medical variety. But he also knows that inventors and early developers of communications and computer technologies often underpredicted both their uses and their impact—sometimes stunningly so in retrospect.

Over twenty years ago, I convened the first conference on computers and the consumer. Even at that time, it was apparent that computers were receiving a highly one-sided application on the side of manufacturers, wholesalers, and retail vendors. The consumer was neither provided direct access to this new tool nor receiving direct benefits such as easily retrievable data on comparative prices, safety, durability, and other product and service data in order to shop more wisely. Indeed, sellers were accumulating more and more data about consumers—medical, credit, buying patterns, etc., which also invaded their privacy.

The still one-sided applications of computers pertain to medicine as well. The inventory, administrative, billing, and patient records sections of hospitals, for example, have computers with more and more complex software to serve the vendors, euphemistically called the providers. Dr. Slack wants the computer programs in these more mundane areas, along with the direct interface between clinicians and patients, to be placed for use by and at the service of patients and their families. A particularly prominent illustration of one-sided computerization is computerized billing fraud and abuse, which one General Accounting Office report estimated to be consuming 10 percent of health care expenditures in this country. Imagine the discipline that would result from more consumer-side use of and access to computerized data and practices in billing, medical malpractice, budgetary allocations between clinical and administrative personnel, and other festering conditions in America's largest industry, which will reach one trillion dollars in 1997.

The human factors approach to technology, as with automotive safety, has registered major declines in mortality and morbidity in recent decades. Dr. Slack believes that enough has now been demonstrated, as described in this book, to warrant an accelerated and comprehensive advance in clinical computing in hospitals and clinics, leading to direct patient and family use of interactive computer programs that have human beings at the other end to ensure the supremacy of the patient's needs. As he writes, "Any doctor who can be replaced by a computer deserves to be." Because computerized business and professional cultures can become interminably fascinating ends in themselves, it is obligatory for practitioners of clinical computing to ask, and measure the results from answering, these questions: "Is the computer helping to improve the quality of medical care? Is the computer helping the patient in matters of health and illness?"

Cybermedicine does not duck the "but" issues; it faces them forthrightly, as in the discussion of privacy and confidentiality. It stresses trying, testing, and revising as built-in cautions against wrongheaded turns or computer hubris.

The growing domination of conglomerate-directed managed care, with its control of practitioners, its deskilling of staff, and its shifting of costs onto the consumer, presents new imperatives for patient empowerment. Enter more home care. In a recent report on the new asthma care guidelines issued by the National Heart, Lung, and Blood Institute of the National Institutes of Health, asthma patients were urged to take more control of their own treatment. "Medicine is a partnership now," said Dr. Shirley Murphy, a professor at the University of New Mexico school of medicine and chairperson of the experts panel. "Patients need to take a greater responsibility for managing their chronic disease." There will be more such urgings for patient self-management.

Notwithstanding its thematic optimism and concrete justifications, *Cybermedicine* does not underestimate the obstacles nor the unintended consequences of interactions between and among computers, clinicians, and patients. There is a long road ahead, in the midst of episodic progress, before this machine and its software are made to adjust to human beings at all levels and backgrounds. This book elevates the discussion and the search for greater heights of public scrutiny and evaluation, and does so in a clear, at times literary, style. And it is style that puts substance on wheels.

Washington, D.C.   RALPH NADER
March 1997

—ᴟᴟ— Preface

When I was in medical school in the late 1950s, I was troubled by the emphasis on memorization. It was as if we novice doctors were expected to keep all the information necessary to practice good medicine in our minds at all times, never forgetting anything for a moment. Notes and reminders were frowned on. I also remember that the *Merck Manual* fit nicely in the pocket of my white jacket and that old Professor Gradgrind accosted me with critical countenance and words of derision for carrying it, as if looking something up were a form of cheating. Yet the professor's professed expectations seemed inconsistent with the workings of the human brain—rapid, reliable recall of a large number of facts is not its forte—so, along with my classmates, I quickly learned to do my looking up in private. (A curious ritual in college had led many of us to pretend we hadn't studied for a test when we really had, in order to appear "intelligent" to our peers.)

It also seemed clear to me that this obsession with memory was not good for patients, particularly since we were destined to work with a rapidly expanding base of information. What if I forgot something? I thought of the airline pilot who was thoroughly familiar with the instruments in the cockpit yet still had to go through a checklist (an aeronautical *Merck Manual*, so to speak) before takeoff and landing. And as a passenger, I was reassured by the process. I decided that I would want my doctor to look things up. It was then that I first had the idea that the computer, which was just coming into being, could be of help to doctors and patients in the future of medicine.

Later, as a resident in neurology and then on the faculty, I had the good fortune to spend the decade of the 1960s at the University of Wisconsin in Madison, where a wonderfully radical atmosphere of strong social conscience and progressive ideology pervaded the campus. Remarkable science was being done there as well. Gobind Khorana was synthesizing a gene in a test tube, Howard Temin was postulating reverse transcriptase in RNA viruses, Milton Yatvin was lending new understanding to the hormonal control of genetic expression, Harry Harlow was elucidating the psychological bonds between mother and infant, and Carl Rogers, in a small, two-story cottage on University Avenue, was developing his theory of nondirective psychotherapy.

It was in this environment that two lines of reasoning evolved in my mind. The first was that the computer could be used wisely and well in the practice of medicine. The electronic digital computer, with its capacity to hold large amounts of data and to execute multiple complex instructions with great speed and accuracy, would, I reasoned, find an important clinical role in both diagnosis and treatment. Why couldn't the computer satisfy the need for facts and free the doctor to spend more time with the existentially important aspects of the doctor-patient relationship?

The second line of reasoning led to a philosophy that I called "patient power," in the vernacular of the times, arguing that patients who want to should be encouraged to make their own clinical decisions and helped to do so. For centuries, the medical profession had perpetrated paternalism as an essential component of medical care, thereby depriving patients of the self-esteem that comes from self-reliance. The assumption was that the doctor knew best. Patient power questioned this assumption. As George Bernard Shaw once wrote, "Do not do unto others as you would that they should do unto you. Their tastes may not be the same."

Like the idea of computers in medicine, the idea of patient power was highly controversial for its time. In 1961, during a visit to our home in Madison, my brother, Charles, took me to meet Carl Rogers, who had introduced the concept of client-centered therapy to clinical psychology. This meeting was one of the turning points in my life. Rogers's support of patient power was the reinforcement I needed to persevere.

Contrary to the prevailing wisdom of the 1960s, the computer was destined to play an important role in patient power. In dialogue with the patient, the computer would be a means of transferring control to the patient, a "patient's assistant" if you will. And in dialogue with the doctor and other clinicians who care for patients, the computer would be a helpful extension of the mind. Contrary to the dire predictions of well-meaning humanists, the computer would have a *humanizing* influence on the practice of medicine.

There were to be two developments that would augment the interaction between patient and computer and between clinician and computer. One was the Internet. I did not know it at the time, but in the 1960s, the seeds of the Internet were beginning to germinate. The other development was the personal computer. During the same thirty-year period, the computer was to evolve from a large, expensive, cumbersome mainframe to a small, affordable, easy-to-use personal machine.

Today, patients with PCs and access to the Internet no longer have to depend on the medical establishment for information on health and disease. They can sign on at any time of day or night, read medical articles, and communicate with other patients. Clinicians are also availing themselves of the medical information available on the Internet and the ability to communicate by electronic mail. Furthermore, clinicians and patients are using electronic mail to communicate with each other, exchanging information and offering advice and suggestions as peers, in a manner unprecedented in the annals of medicine. This is patient power at work, fostered by computer technology.

My argument in this book is that computer programs that help patients and doctors with medical matters can both improve the quality and reduce the cost of medical care. Programs that help the doctor practice medicine can also improve the quality of the doctor's working life. In addition, good clinical computing can improve the relationship between the patient and doctor.

Yet good clinical computing is still more the exception than the rule, particularly where bureaucracy prevails. Ironically, with the burgeoning technology of worldwide communications, doctors and patients often have more computing available to them outside the walls of their medical institutions than inside them.

In spite of the great advances in computer technology, the clinician, the patient, and the prospective patient have yet to realize the full benefit of these machines. There are of course real dangers with the misuse of the computer, such as true dehumanization, depersonalization, and breach of privacy, and we must keep our guard up. On balance, however, the problem is not too much automation in medicine; the problem is *too little.*

In the pages that follow, I discuss my experience with computers in medicine over the past thirty-five years. And on the basis of this experience, I offer suggestions for the future. This is not a review of *medical informatics*, as the study of computers in medicine is often called. I refer only briefly to the work of others, although I am well aware that my voice is but one among many. This is one individual's account, based on personal experience. If my experiences with clinical computing produce even a little optimism in your mind about the future of medicine, an important goal will have been accomplished. And if you come to realize what the forces of bureaucracy are doing to reduce the quality of that future—and what clinicians and concerned patients can have if they insist on computing that puts their interests ahead of administrative careerism—then my book will have served its purpose.

ACKNOWLEDGMENTS

I am deeply indebted to my parents, Evelyn and Charles, my children—Alison, Charles (who did the cartoons for the book), and Jennifer—and their families, and most of all my wife, Carolyn, for all their help and support.

I want to give special thanks to Bill Adler, my very helpful agent, Alan Rinzler, my excellent editor at Jossey-Bass, and most of all, Emily Boro, managing editor of *M.D. Computing*. Emily has been of invaluable help to me with my writing over the years. She has edited the articles from *M.D. Computing* that I have incorporated into my book, and she has helped me in immeasurable ways with the entire manuscript.

I am greatly indebted to John Cameron, Frank Larson, and Robert Schilling of the University of Wisconsin, Raymond Keating of the Mayo Clinic, and Alvan R. Feinstein of Yale University School of Medicine for their support and guidance in my early years of clinical computing. And I am greatly indebted to Mitchell T. Rabkin, president, and David Dolins, executive vice president, of Boston's Beth Israel Hospital, and Richard Nesson, president, and Anthony Komaroff, director of the Division of General Medicine, of Brigham and Women's Hospital, for inviting us into their hospitals and supporting our work in clinical computing.

I am particularly grateful to Howard Hiatt, an early staunch supporter of clinical computing at Harvard Medical School and my esteemed mentor over the years; to my brother, Charles, my best friend and valued colleague; and to Howard Bleich, my partner for over twenty-five years and a true pioneer in clinical computing.

And finally, I am indebted to my friends and colleagues at the Center for Clinical Computing, Beth Israel Hospital, Brigham and Women's Hospital, Harvard Medical School, and the University of Wisconsin, for their many contributions to the work described in this book.

Boston, Mass.
January 1997

WARNER V. SLACK, M.D.

Cybermedicine

PART ONE

The Computer and the Patient

"I THINK THERE IS A WORLD MARKET FOR MAYBE FIVE COMPUTERS."
THOMAS WATSON, CHAIRMAN, IBM, 1943

"I FORESEE THE NEED FOR ABOUT FIVE HUMANS."

CHAPTER ONE

Providing Information to Patients

⁓ I t can be argued that the largest yet most neglected health care resource, worldwide, is the patient or prospective patient. Most people could readily manage a number of common, important medical problems, such as sore throat, urinary tract infection, and headache, if provided with the clinical information necessary to do so. I don't mean to suggest that self-care can be accomplished by taking Hygiene 101 from the basketball coach in his spare time—or by studying Molecular Biology 401, with a discourse on the genetic determinants of immunological mechanisms. I mean good, solid, reliable, up-to-date, best current wisdom that virtually any literate person who wants to can understand.

Until recently, communication between doctor and patient was for the most part one-way—the doctor ordered and the patient was expected to obey. The "good" patient followed orders dutifully; the noncompliant (read "bad") patient didn't. But times are changing; not as fast as we might like, but changing for the better.

Doctors should give people sufficient information to enable them, or their designated surrogates, to make enlightened decisions about matters of health and disease. People should know how they can best achieve and preserve good health and the good health of their families. They should know when a problem is not a medical problem—when, for example, the sadness that follows the loss of a loved one is healthy grief that will abate with time, and when it is clinical depression that could benefit from counseling or medication. They should know when to care for a medical problem themselves and how best to do this—for example, how to care for a laceration that is too small for stitches (lots of soap and water; no iodine).

People also need to know when it would be better to turn to others for help and how and where to do so. What are often the most difficult of diagnostic decisions typically get left to the patient—when to consult a doctor, which doctor to consult, and how to get in touch. When, for example, is the laceration big enough for stitches, and where should the stitching be done? In other words, people need to know what to do in a medical emergency.

HOW DOCTORS TALK TO PATIENTS

There are a number of ways in which doctors can help people become better informed about matters of health and disease. The oldest and in many ways still the most effective medium is face-to-face communication. This works best one on one or in small groups, where questions can be asked, answers given, and ideas exchanged—an interpersonal medium where the doctor as well as the patient can become better informed. Of course individual attention is not always possible, and when it is, it can be very expensive.

What then are some good ways to communicate medical information in the absence of direct interpersonal communication?

Early Technology

Since early times, growth in population has been accompanied by innovation in communication, inventions that enhance the exchange of information among larger and larger groups of people, but that do so at the expense of direct interpersonal conversation. Each invention, impersonal by its very nature, has in turn been subject to early criticism both by the well-meaning humanist who objects to anything seen as having a depersonalizing influence, and by the well-meaning traditionalist, who opposes innovation on principle. I suspect that when the person who invented writing first carved those primordial symbols in stone along the Nile Valley some five thousand years ago, a skeptic standing nearby predicted with furrowed brow that people would soon stop *talking* to each other. Those who read the *Republic* in school will remember that Plato was very much opposed to theater as it was performed in ancient Greece. For him the portrayal of fictional characters was an ignoble pursuit that exposed audiences to the risk of corruption.

In more modern times, the telephone was written off prematurely: according to an internal memorandum at Western Union in 1876, the telephone "has too many shortcomings to be seriously considered as a means of communication. The device is inherently of no value to us." The motion picture was also greeted with suspicion. The stage was by then a reputable medium ("legitimate theater," as it were), but the movie, even as it gained in popularity, was deemed vulgar and dangerous. To make a movie based on a book was a priori to debase the book. Parents worried about bad cinematic influences and meted out movie-going privileges with extreme judiciousness. Dorothy Parker likened the movie to sex, pointing out that while many enjoyed it, few talked about it.

Radio had a similar history. "The wireless music box has no imaginable commercial value. Who would pay for a message sent to nobody in particular?" argued David Sarnoff's associates in the 1920s, when he urged them to support radio as a commercial venture. Popular as it was to become, radio was late to be accepted publicly by the intelligentsia. *The Green Hornet, Captain Midnight, Terry and the Pirates,* and *Superman* (together with their comic book counterparts) were intermittently banned from middle-class households. Kids, of course, still listened—but did so in the protective design of youthful subterfuge.

After World War II came television—lowbrow (boxing and wrestling were the staple programs) and potentially corrupting. As television broadened its scope and became increasingly available and popular, it was correspondingly chic among the culturati *not* to have television at home. There was a family in our neighborhood in the 1970s who did not have a set in their home. Mention of television in conversation with the parents elicited blank faces. Their children, however, spent an inordinate amount of time in front of *our* set.

Movies and radio were by then regarded as legitimate art forms, particularly the earlier, pre–World War II films and programs. It was soon acceptable to consider a movie *better* than the book on which it was based (*The Godfather* was an example).

The personal computer is the new medium on the block. And once again, prophecy was off the mark. "I think there is a world market for maybe five computers," Thomas Watson, chairman of IBM, is purported to have said in 1943. But I am getting ahead of myself.

Medicine and the Printed Word

When Johannes Gutenberg invented the printing press in the mid-fifteenth century, he used his invention to publish the first printed version of the Christian Bible. His machine would have an enormous influence on secular communication, although the medical profession was slow to adopt the printed word as a means of communication with patients. Patients were to be kept in the dark, knowing only what their doctors wanted them to know. Information in the hands of the patient could be dangerous, it was believed. When the doctor handed the patient a prescription it was written in Latin to *prevent* communication. Well into the twentieth century, medical articles in the popular press were treated at best with amusement by the profession. This reluctance to go public with professional secrets is not unique to medicine. Most professions are protective of their information, which serves to differentiate them from the public. Scientists who write for the public risk criticism from their peers; only giants such as Einstein can write for the nonscientist without at least some risk of reprisal from the scientific priesthood. To this day, doctors who write for the public are suspected of publicity seeking, of pandering to the public and jeopardizing patients, for whom a little knowledge might be a dangerous thing indeed. The concern that the public will not understand and will be misled is certainly legitimate, but it is sometimes expressed as a covert means of protecting the guild, rather than the public. There is valuable equity in the concentration of information.

In 1946 came a turning point in medical publications for the public. Pocket Books published *Baby and Child Care*, by Benjamin Spock. Criticized at first by the American Medical Association and the American Psychological Association—for pandering to the public, being too permissive in approach, and definitely *not* representing Park Avenue pediatrics—Spock's book so obviously filled a niche that it could not be stifled. It told how to care for a sick baby at 2 A.M.; it told parents when they could care for the baby at home and when to call a doctor, when to worry and when *not* to worry. Parents might not discuss Spock's advice at a seminar on psychological theory or at a golf club social, but there was no way that *anyone* was going to wrest Spock's book from their hands when their child was sick. It has been estimated that *Baby and Child Care* is second only to the Bible in total sales. Spock legitimized the medical book for the public, and publications on self-care are now published in abundance, many even with the blessing of the AMA. The old adage, "the person who treats himself has a fool for a doctor," is being replaced by titles such as *How to Be Your Own Doctor.*

Yet the published forum, like the lecture, is still a type of one-way communication. There is little provision for interaction with the author or lecturer. In addition, it can be hard to assess the accuracy of published material, particularly if there is disagreement among experts, which is often the case in the medical profession (more often than we care to acknowledge). When there is disagreement, whose advice does the reader follow? One cannot turn readily to the writer and ask for evidence. Still, a book can be kept close at hand, available for quick reference whenever needed, at any time of day or night.

As self-help books and articles on medical matters appear at an accelerating rate, their success creates a bewildering surfeit. The problem now is how to select the ones that can be trusted. And most of us cannot afford to house large libraries in our homes. Even when a good book is at hand, it is often hard to locate the page or chapter that meets the needs of the moment; the index and table of contents may be confusing.

Like all communications media except face-to-face conversation, the book is impersonal; the author is separated from the reader. The ideal would be to have Dr. Spock in conversation in the living room. But to have his words of wisdom on the printed page, close at hand, is a very good second best, impersonal as it may be. Books are portable and are usually replaceable if lost or worn out. The first-aid manual is here to stay, at least in the foreseeable future. Still, there are problems for the health-minded reader.

The Airwaves

Perhaps recognizing the problems of books, a few doctors have turned to the airwaves, sometimes reluctantly and sometimes with zeal. As far back as 1936, CBS radio aired a fifteen-minute child health program, hosted by Dr. Alan Roy Dafoe, the physician who delivered the Dionne quintuplets. But radio and television are still basically one-way communicators over which the listener has little control. With medical topics, it is the producer, not the patient, who schedules the programming. A diabetic in need of immediate advice is not going to tune in a lengthy discussion of glucose metabolism on public television if a booklet from the American Diabetes Association is on the bedside table.

In some radio and television programs, however, the listener or viewer can converse with the expert over the telephone. This type of talk show is a response, I'm convinced, to the frustration evoked by one-way communication. People are restless by nature; they like to interact. They can take just so much of Pat Robertson without wanting to talk back. (If you're itching to talk back to *me* at this moment, you can use my electronic mail address: wslack@bih.harvard.edu.) And sit-still behavior does not come naturally. The ever-proliferating cellular phone (ubiquitous on streets from Sydney to Paris) is another example of the guy on the street talking back.

The audience participation talk show was invented, almost certainly, not by a clever producer but by an irate listener who demanded the opportunity to get a word in, albeit edgewise. Sports and politics, the first call-in topics, still dominate the airwaves, but medicine has found its dial-in niche, whereby doctors can give specific advice to callers. On midday television in Boston, Timothy Johnson takes "house calls" on medical matters, Tom Cottle counsels troubled callers on psychological issues, and Alexis Beck gives advice on nutrition. In San Francisco, Dean Edell offers medical common sense on both radio and television call-in shows. Helpful as these programs may be, however, they still serve mainly as forums of general interest, rather than solutions to the specific medical needs of patients. The waiting time for callers is long, often as long as the time in the physician's waiting room, few callers get on the air, and air time is short.

WHEN PATIENTS TALK WITH PATIENTS

In 1935, Bill W., a recovering alcoholic, found himself in Akron, Ohio, the victim of a failed business venture. Fearful that he might have a relapse, Bill had a remarkable insight—if he wanted to help himself, he should find and help another alcoholic. He found Dr. Bob, an alcoholic physician, and helped him to stop drinking. It was there, in Akron, that Bill W. and Dr. Bob (neither of whom ever drank again) founded Alcoholics Anonymous, the most successful approach to alcoholism ever devised.

Bill W.'s insight, that one's own experience with a medical problem can be used to help someone else with the same problem, and that in doing this, one is helping oneself, is at the heart of all successful self-help and medical support programs. Only an alcoholic can fully understand the experience of alcoholism. Only a woman who has undergone chemotherapy for breast cancer herself can fully understand what is in store for another woman with the same diagnosis. The parents of a toddler with diabetes will know what this entails—the blood tests, insulin injections, meal planning, and day-to-day living, at home and in the outside world. And in communicating their experiences to help others, these people are putting their problems to good use in what I think is the most durable form of altruism—helping yourself while helping others. Sadly, the self-help programs in their early days were sometimes treated with scorn by the medical profession. But doctors are coming to realize, however belatedly, that all of us—patient and clinician alike—can benefit from the principle that patients and their families are an invaluable resource for helping themselves while helping others. It's enlightened self-interest in the best sense of the words.

Initiated not by clinical experts but by people who share the same problem, symbiotic communication has seen remarkable growth over the past sixty years. More and more, people are sharing their problems and their strategies for coping, both formally and informally, one on one, in groups, forums, books, and pamphlets, and on radio and television. It is the wise doctor who knows when *not* to intrude on such beneficial communication.

ON-THE-SPOT INSTRUCTION

It is helpful to differentiate between information that we have committed to memory and information not in our memory but readily available through external sources. In the classroom, where great emphasis is placed on memory, external sources of information are suspect. Teachers worry about the handheld calculator or the use of crib notes during an examination. Outside the classroom, however, memory is less important. If information is on hand whenever needed—for example, how to start the furnace, how to place the jump start cables, or, on a more esoteric level, how to calculate the area under a curve—there is little need to memorize. There are even good reasons not to rely on memory.

Rapid, reliable recall is not always a strength of the human mind, for all its marvelous attributes. It is often safer to read instructions than to rely on memory, particularly when the information is important but rarely used. Paradoxically, if the information is often used, this too can result in errors. When the familiarity of a protocol leads to boredom, our minds tend to wander. When the stakes are high, as in the cockpit of a commercial airplane about to take off, the copilot reads a checklist to the pilot, even though the pilot knows the panel by heart.

And so it is in medicine, at least for the patient if not the doctor. Doctors tend to be obsessed with memory (knowing it all can be a matter of pride), but patients do not need to memorize medical information. They just need to have it handy. Better to have the first-aid manual readily available than to commit its contents to memory.

ENTER THE COMPUTER

The essence of the computer, in contrast to the book, play, movie, radio, or television, is its ability to *interact*, to converse with its user one on one. As a prescription for the patient, the computer can be programmed to simulate one-on-one conversation, but with the collective wisdom of many doctors.

The idea of a patient "talking" to a computer was hotly debated at its inception in the radical decade of the 1960s and is still controversial. This is understandable. Novelty is unsettling. It is hard for us to assess the potential, for good or for bad, of a new idea. This is true in virtually all walks of life—the arts, the sciences, the professions, and the marketplace. Good ideas are often thwarted—as Machiavelli observed, "The innovator makes enemies of all those who prospered under the old order."

And so it has been in medicine. On the one hand, René Laënnec was ridiculed for his invention of the stethoscope (it separated the doctor's ear from the patient's chest, for one thing), and Ignaz Semmelweis couldn't convince his fellow Viennese obstetricians to wash their hands before delivery. On the other hand, bad ideas are often promulgated. Carcinogenic X rays were once used to treat normal thymus glands, ringworm, and acne; tonsillectomies were routinely performed under general anesthesia in healthy children; and the operation to remove the frontal lobes of the brain (prefrontal lobotomy) was a common treatment for mental illness.

And so it has been with the invention of the computer and its introduction to society and medicine.

BREAKING THE ICE WITH A LITTLE HUMOR

CHAPTER TWO

The First
Patient-Computer
Dialogue

—‑⁀‑ The first patient to "talk" to a computer did so at the
University of Wisconsin Hospitals in 1965. At the time, my goal with
the computer in medicine was to help the doctor with diagnosis and
treatment. It was clear from the start, however, that if the computer
was to help with the care of a patient, good information about the
patient would have to be available to the computer—for example, the
medical history, obtained from an interview with the patient, the physical examination, obtained by the doctor, and the results of diagnostic studies, obtained from the laboratory. My office mate, Philip Hicks,
was working to automate the laboratories; I decided to start with the
medical history. In collaboration with Phil, Lawrence Van Cura, and
other colleagues, I hypothesized that we could program a computer
to take a medical history directly from a patient.

Our motivation came in part from a theoretical question: Could a
computer be programmed to engage in meaningful dialogue with a
patient? Could it actually interview a patient? There were also practical motives. The traditional method of taking and recording medical
histories involved serious problems for the busy clinician, particularly
in areas of our country that were short on doctors. Asking a lot of

questions takes a lot of time, and incomplete histories frequently resulted from time limitations beyond the doctor's control. Northern Wisconsin was short of doctors; for those who were seeing up to thirty or forty patients a day, there was barely enough time to ask "Where does it hurt?"—let alone all the other questions in the standard interview. Furthermore, recording the results of a medical interview in longhand was a laborious process, and histories were often nonstandardized, incomplete, and illegibly written—characteristics that greatly hampered the subsequent use of this information in patient care and clinical research.

In the 1960s, self-administered paper questionnaires were being used with considerable success; the Cornell Medical Index and the "multiphasic" questionnaire of the Permanente Medical Group provided standardized, consistent, and inexpensive methods for taking medical histories. Furthermore, the Cornell and Permanente systems used a computer to process the responses—one of the first applications of the computer in medicine. And many good self-administered medical questionnaires are used throughout the country today. Questionnaires, however, cannot be tailored to the particular needs of the individual because they permit no interaction. They provide no mechanism either to clarify the meaning of a question or to qualify the answer. If the respondent answers the question "Have you had any pain in your chest?" with yes, it could mean a minor ache of no consequence or an important sign of impending heart trouble. The respondent might misunderstand a question (and thereby give an erroneous answer), inadvertently skip a question, or lose one or more pages of the questionnaire. Furthermore, filling out questionnaires is drudgery for most people.

Our idea was to incorporate into the computer program at least some of the advantages of the physician as an interviewer: the ability to explore abnormal findings in detail and to personalize the interview in an appropriate, dignified, and considerate manner. At the same time, we wanted to gain the advantages of the questionnaire: its completeness, standardization, and economy.

We hoped that the computer-based interview would be helpful to the doctor in the care of the patient, that using the computer would be of interest to the patient (perhaps even enjoyable), and that pooled responses from many interviews would help us to learn more about the importance of the questions in the interview and to study the process of clinical interviewing. In addition to thinking about using computers in hospitals, clinics, and physicians' offices, I had the idea of a "medical history mobile," similar to the chest X-ray mobile of the era, that would serve prospective patients in remote parts of our country. And in the back of my mind was the idea that perhaps the computer could actually help patients help themselves.

BEGINNINGS OF PATIENT-COMPUTER DIALOGUE

Some of our colleagues considered the idea radical. Those who questioned the use of the computer in medicine under any circumstances were particularly concerned about the use of a machine to take a medical history—a time-honored traditional interaction between doctor and patient, hallowed ground in Western medicine. Some said it could not be done; others wondered if it *should* be done. Still others said that patients would find the idea offensive and would refuse to be interviewed by a computer, regardless of the nature of the program. (Years later, in completion of the critic's circle, they would ask, "Isn't everybody doing it?")

Patients, however, were remarkably enthusiastic. "It sounds like fun" and "I'd like to try my hand with a computer" were typical responses, particularly if (as was most often the case in 1965) they had never seen a computer. Their one concern was that the computer might try to perform an "intelligence test"—they didn't seem to like intelligence tests. I assured them that I didn't either, and that I certainly did not want our computer to do intelligence testing. If anything, I wanted the computer to *do away* with intelligence testing. They seemed relieved.

Starting with "A," I picked allergies for our first computer-based history. This seemed like a neutral, inoffensive subject for a computer; it is a field of great medical importance that relies heavily on the medical history, and our allergist consultant, Charles Reed, gave his enthusiastic support. We also mistakenly thought that an allergy history would be short. By the time we called a halt to expansion there were over five hundred questions in the program.

Enter the LINC

Philip Hicks suggested that we use the LINC (laboratory instrument computer) for our study. He was already using the LINC to develop his programs, the first of their kind, for use in the clinical laboratories at the University of Wisconsin Hospitals. This small, general-purpose digital computer was developed at the Massachusetts Institute of Technology in 1962 by Wesley Clark, Charles Molnar, and their colleagues; it was a pioneering machine, and in many respects was the forerunner of today's personal computers.

Flexibility and ease of operation were stressed in the development of the LINC. With it, the individual user could exert maximum control over the computer—a major departure from the batch-processing brontosaurs of the day. Designed to interact with the environment, the LINC was equipped with relays, sense switches, sense lines, analog-to-digital conversion channels (converting electronic signals such as wave forms to numbers), toggle switches, a cathode-ray oscilloscope that could double as a display screen, a typewriter keyboard, and a teletype printer.

Thus the LINC was well suited for *on-line* collection (that is, collection of data directly by the computer) and *real-time* processing (processing data as fast as they are generated). It found widespread use in neurophysiology laboratories, where it could be programmed to study the electrical activity of the nervous system—to initiate stimuli, receive responses, and then alter subsequent stimuli contingent upon the nature of the responses received. This was a hands-on computer; the wires were all hanging out, so to speak. There were no computing committees or subcommittees, no director of computing or chief information officer, no Mr. Binary telling you to keep out or not to touch. Users loved it!

Our plan was to program the LINC to communicate with the patient by means of questions, explanations, requests, and comments displayed on the cathode-ray screen. The patient, in turn, could communicate with the computer by means of the typewriter keyboard. The LINC had a very small memory by today's standards—1,024 twelve-bit words—barely enough to hold the text for one question, together with the instructions in the program that told the computer what to do. The off-the-shelf personal computer of today brings with it at least eight million bytes of memory—about four thousand times as much memory as the LINC. The memory wasn't a crippling limitation, however—two magnetic tape drives, which could turn equally well in either direction, provided storage space for additional text and instructions that could quickly be called into memory when needed.

The LINC was also slow by today's standards, and the time between iterative instructions that told the computer to display a character on the screen—time in which the computer was executing other instructions, such as commands to display other characters—resulted in a flicker that became increasingly noticeable as the number of characters increased. There was reason, therefore, to keep the questions short, and this electronically imposed succinctness had a beneficial effect on the quality of my prose.

We used one of the original LINCs, which had been brought to the University of Wisconsin's neurophysiology laboratory by Joseph Hind. The machine was in great demand, and programming time during the day was scarce; we did most of our work between 10 P.M. and 8 A.M. Within a few months we had the program written and working well, but found ourselves continuing to make revisions. Most of these were minor and, in retrospect, inconsequential, and eventually I had to own up to the fact that I was procrastinating. It had been fun to talk about a computer that could take a medical history, to shock the traditionalists, and to argue with the skeptics, but to try it with a real patient— *for the first time*—that was another matter.

The First Patient

The time came, however, when I decided it was now or never. I approached one of our medical interns and asked him if he could select a patient for me. He seemed amused by the idea; he was tired— he had been up all night, as part of the draconian tradition in American medicine that doctors in training should go without sleep—and the thought of being replaced by a computer, at least at night, had a distinct appeal. He suggested a patient who might be willing to help, an elderly man who was recovering from a heart attack and was now up and about, getting ready to go home. I went to his room, introduced myself, told him the general idea of the project, explained that I didn't know how well it would work, and asked if he would give us a hand. "I'll try anything once," he replied, and he walked with me to the medical sciences building, where the LINC was housed. Fortunately, there was a free hour at lunchtime for us to try our first interview. Game as he was, I couldn't have expected our volunteer to visit the computer at 2 A.M. I turned on the machine, spun in the program from tape, turned off the lights in the room (the dim characters on the screen were easier to read in the dark), pressed the start button, and stepped back to observe.

This was not a randomized, controlled, double-blind experiment, suitable for statistical analysis. It was more like cultural anthropology. In the tradition of Margaret Mead, I had put a machine in the clinical village, and stood by as unobtrusively as possible to see what would happen. Werner Heisenberg once noted that in science, the process of observation itself tends to influence the variables under scrutiny and thereby influence the findings. He derived his famous Uncertainty Principle from observations in physics, but the problem of uncertainty is nowhere more apparent than in the social sciences. The psychologist in the inner city, the criminologist in the federal prison, the anthropologist in the Third World village, and I in the LINC room, by our very presence, tend to affect the activities we hope to examine, and thus stand to compromise our own results. But in this instance, in the LINC room, my volunteer seemed truly oblivious to my presence.

The tapes churned, and "HAVE YOU EVER HAD HIVES?" appeared on the screen. The characters flickered, the lights on the console flashed on and off, and the LINC's speaker emitted an eerie, high-pitched sound. On the other side of the sheetrock partition, people were walking in and out, and a cat was meowing. We had the computer, but its owners were still doing a cat brain experiment. It was somewhat like Kafka's *Castle* or Koestler's *Darkness at Noon*. Clearly, these were not optimal circumstances for *any* medical interview, let alone one conducted by a computer.

Yet my newfound friend seemed oblivious to his surroundings. He got going at the keyboard, responding appropriately to the questions, and after a while it became clear that there was rapport between man and machine. He laughed out loud at some of the comments from the computer. Some I had intended to be funny; some I hadn't. And he talked out loud to the machine, sometimes in praise and sometimes in criticism. "That was a dumb question," he noted with a taunting laugh. "You already asked me that!" He was right, of course; it was my error, although I rationalized that we could use the results, psychometrically, to check for test-retest reliability. He never would have said this to me face to face, a doctor with a white coat and a Bakelite nametag.

For most patients, even today, the doctor presents an authoritarian figure. By contrast, the computer did not seem at all authoritarian to this man; he was comfortable with it and felt free to be frank, even critical. At the conclusion of the interview, he turned to me and said, "You know, I really like your computer better than some of those doctors over in the hospital."

Surprised, I asked him why.

"Well, for one thing, I'm sort of deaf and have trouble hearing them," he answered.

The Patient's Chart Declassified

For each of the possible responses to the computer's questions, we had developed phrases that could be printed when applicable. To appease those colleagues who clung to professional mystique, we converted words such as *hives* and *hay fever* to *urticaria* and *allergic rhinitis*. The computer was programmed to print these phrases—in a legible but otherwise traditional format—as a summary for use by the doctor.

When our first patient had completed his interview, I was relieved to hear the teletype chatter as it began to print; the summary program was working. He then turned to me and said, "What's happening? May I read that?" I could not think of any reason why he shouldn't. Once again, the computer was helping him to assert himself as a patient.

This may have been the first time that any patient at the University of Wisconsin Hospitals was offered the opportunity to read his own record. As he started to read, he commented suddenly, in reference to some details about his hay fever: "No, that's wrong; I didn't mean that," and he then proceeded to pick out other errors. Clearly, there were mistakes in the interview. Yet if he hadn't asked to read his summary, I might never have known.

We learned our lesson, and since that time have asked our patients, whenever they are willing, to read their summaries, help us edit their medical histories, and thereby improve our computer-based interviews. And patients' criticisms have been most helpful over the years. Whether we are writing at a keyboard or in longhand, it is unrealistic and often demeaning to record what patients tell us without letting them see what we've written, and when doctors do so they perpetuate errors that could be corrected. Furthermore, there is a natural tendency to find fault with the patient when difficulties arise; diagnoses such as "inadequate personality" would have disappeared quickly if patients had seen them early on. It seemed clear to me at the time that for patients who want to be active participants in their medical care, the medical record should be declassified as quickly as possible.

A Formal Study

Encouraged by the results of this first interview, we did a more formal study. Fifty hospitalized patients agreed to have their allergy histories taken. In each case, we compared the results of the computer's history as printed out on the teletype with the allergy history as recorded in the hospital chart by the medical student, intern, resident, and staff physician who were caring for the patient.

In medical parlance, because of the traditional orientation to disease rather than health, a *positive* finding denotes the presence of a disease and a *negative* finding denotes its absence. There were no "false negative" findings with the computer interview—that is, the computer interview identified all the allergies mentioned in the patients' charts.

Among patients whose charts gave no indication of allergies, the computer elicited two cases of asthma, seven cases of hay fever, twelve cases of hives, and one case of allergy to penicillin. In this instance, the medical student's workup did mention a rash in association with penicillin, but to find it one had to read the workup from beginning to end; the intern's note stated "no allergies." With another patient, the mention of "penicillin allergy" in the chart was insufficient to determine whether an allergy actually existed, whereas the computer described the single reaction in detail and left no doubt that a serious serum-sickness type of reaction had occurred and that this person should be advised never to take penicillin again. All adverse drug reactions were described in more detail by the computer than by the students and doctors.

On the other hand, the computer elicited and printed out several "false positive" findings, such as an "allergic reaction" to phenobarbital that the patient later described as "excessive grogginess," not an allergy.

At the end of the interview, the computer asked each patient what he or she had thought of the experience. As we had hoped, almost all the patients found their interaction with the computer both interesting and enjoyable. When asked to compare the computer interviews with interviews conducted by doctors, twenty patients had no preference, twelve indicated a preference for physician-taken histories, and—to our surprise—eighteen indicated a preference for the computer-based system. It should be noted, however, that the computer was asking this question. If a doctor had asked about preference, the results might have been different.

Further Studies in Madison and Boston

Heartened by these early results, we pressed on with further studies of computer-based medical interviews in our laboratories at the University of Wisconsin and, more recently, at Beth Israel Hospital in Boston. We developed and studied histories for patients with problems such as cancer, epilepsy, and headache. The uterine cancer interview, which was written by Ben Peckham, his colleagues, and me, asked questions about pregnancies, menstruation, bleeding, and past gynecological procedures. Most patients indicated that they found their time at the computer to be both worthwhile and interesting, and that they had a slight preference for the computer as an interviewer in comparison with physicians in their experience. Once again, however, the computer was doing the asking.

The topics in this interview were of a sensitive, personal nature. It was particularly interesting to me, therefore, to hear from the women who had taken the interview, which was done in private, that they had been more comfortable while communicating information to the computer about potentially embarrassing matters, such as sexual activity, than they would have been while talking to their doctor. Even when they wanted the physician to receive the information, as would be the case when the doctor read the computer's printed summary, they found it easier to tell it to the machine. This observation, which we first reported in 1968, has since been corroborated in a number of studies in a variety of settings.

With the interview for patients with epilepsy, Raymond Chun and I compared the computer's printed summaries with the handwritten summaries of residents and staff physicians, and found that the computer's summaries contained more information about the patients' symptoms before, during, and after their seizures. Again, patients reacted favorably to the computer interview.

The study of the headache interview was done in collaboration with Alan Leviton and his colleagues Dhirendra Bana and John Graham from the Headache Research Foundation in Boston. The forty patients who participated found the interview to be interesting, thoughtful, and considerate. Thirty-eight found the computer program easy to use, but only twenty-two thought that the computer had been complete in taking the history of their headaches. Clearly, additions and revisions were in order.

Six internists and one neurologist, each with a strong interest in headache studies, reviewed the printed summaries of these computer histories and incorporated them into their clinical evaluations. For twenty-two of these patients, the physicians indicated that the summaries had been helpful in their evaluations; for seven patients, the computer had clarified the nature of the headache, and for five patients, the computer had provided information that was not available in the personal history. In most instances, the physicians indicated that they would like to use the computer's summaries in the future.

When we analyzed patients' responses to the computer and compared them with physicians' diagnoses, we found that precursors of headaches, such as changes in vision, changes in weather, and consumption of alcohol, which are generally believed to be unique to the diagnosis of migraine, were almost as frequent among patients with muscle contraction or tension headache. We concluded that muscle contraction headache is more similar to migraine than is generally recognized.

At the same time, we were working to develop a comprehensive computer-based general medical history—a complete history for all seasons and all situations. It started with a rudimentary review of body systems, such as the heart, lungs, and abdomen, branching to a few questions for qualification of each abnormality. Over the years, we have revised this history, made it more detailed in some areas and less detailed in others, and (in collaboration with Guerdon Coombs and Patricia Downs) modified it to the needs of individual clinics, such as the Marshfield Clinic in rural Wisconsin and the Harvard Street Clinic in Boston—where it was translated into French and Spanish to accommodate patients who had recently immigrated from Haiti and Puerto Rico.

SPREADING THE WORD

In the meantime, others began to work in the field. A general medical history, with emphasis on the review of systems, was developed and studied at the Mayo Clinic, and both patients and physicians reacted favorably. The computer obtained 95 percent of the information about the symptoms that had been recorded in the traditional medical record. Another general medical history was studied at the Massachusetts General Hospital, where patients reacted favorably. Physicians' attitudes were mixed, but the computer's summaries were in good agreement with the physicians' findings. A general medical history was also studied at LDS Hospital in Salt Lake City. With this history, Bayes's theorem—a mathematical technique to estimate the likelihood of different outcomes—was used to make diagnostic suggestions on the basis of patients' responses to the computer. Meanwhile, other investigators were developing and evaluating histories in psychiatry and psychology, nutrition, headache, venereal disease, and allergy. In 1994, Jonathan Wald, with his coworkers at our Center for Clinical Computing, introduced a computer-based medical interview in Beth Israel Hospital's ambulatory care facility. The interview has been well received by patients and clinicians alike.

Research in the field of computer-based interviewing remains active to this day. Patient-computer dialogue is not as yet readily available in most clinical settings, but I am optimistic that it will be in the not too distant future.

The Patient in Control

The idea of a computer taking a medical history can evoke worrisome thoughts: *2001: A Space Odyssey, Terminal Man, Invasion of the Body Snatchers*, Orwellian thought control. Yet the experience of our first patient, and the majority of patients who have subsequently engaged in dialogue with our computers, was the opposite of what some had predicted. This man had *gained* control, not lost it. For the first time in his role as a patient, *he* was in charge; he was master of his own history. And in his world of deafness he could communicate particularly well with the machine.

Patient Power

In the spring of 1970, I discussed my ideas on patient power at a conference at the University of Michigan in Ann Arbor. Those in attendance were divided in their reaction, and the ensuing debate was heated. The moderator, John Romano (chair of the Department of Psychiatry at the University of Rochester) staunchly defended the right of the physician to direct the patient ("patients want to be told what to do"); Leonard Savage (professor of statistics at Yale), on the other hand, said that he "was particularly pleased to hear the bold and radical defense of the thesis that medical values should be those of the patient."

The debate was to continue through the 1970s. Franz Ingelfinger, editor of the *New England Journal of Medicine*, rejected my article "The Patient's Right to Decide," making it clear that he strongly disagreed with my position. On the other hand, Ian Monroe, editor of the *Lancet* (to whom I will be forever grateful), sent me an encouraging letter of acceptance and published my article forthwith. But all agreed during those decades of debate that when it came to dialogue between patient and computer, the patient should be in charge. Ironically, it would be easier to transfer control to the patient by means of an automaton than by means of the physician.

THE MECHANICS OF THE INTERVIEW

The power of the computer as an interviewing machine is in its *branching*, that is, moving from frame (or display) to frame in a manner contingent on the patient's responses. In this way the computer can ask questions, answer questions in turn, teach the meaning of concepts not understood, give advice and suggestions, and provide words of encouragement, even with a bit of humor here and there. As I gained experience in writing interviews, I found myself better able to use the power of this new medium to personalize the dialogue and transfer control from the computer to the person engaged in dialogue with the computer.

The Dialogue

Typically, the patient interacts with the computer by means of the screen and keyboard on a computer terminal, or more recently, on a personal computer. The computer communicates with the patient by means of text displayed on the screen, and the patient communicates with the computer by means of the keyboard. If a person is blind or illiterate, a surrogate can read the questions on the screen.

There have been several studies using a prerecorded or computer-generated voice to present the questions. Such techniques have promise, particularly when used in telephone interviews, as in the programs of Lee Baer and his colleagues, because the telephone is more readily available than the personal computer. If the person is deaf, however, voice is unusable unless a surrogate is available to sign. Computers that can recognize the spoken word have great potential for the future, but for the present, they are not generally available—and in any case, most models have limited vocabularies.

With our programs, the dialogue between computer and patient usually begins with words of welcome. "Hello! It's good to be 'talking' with you today. To begin, please press the 'Enter' key on the keyboard." If the patient does so, the computer continues: "Exactly, pressing 'Enter' is the way to continue. Why not try it again?" And, if "Enter" is pressed again, the computer responds with "You have a nice touch with the keys." This typically elicits a bit of laughter, and the interview is under way.

The dialogue then continues with instruction on how to use the keyboard. The patient must be able to read the frames on the screen, and be capable of sustained mental activity, to interact with the computer during the introductory and teaching sections. If all goes well with these beginning frames, the patient is probably ready for the medical questions. If the patient cannot negotiate the opening sequences, this is a good indication that personal intervention is warranted.

Over the years, we have incorporated into our programs a number of provisions designed to yield control to the patient in dialogue with the computer. With the typical interview, we request permission to proceed (for example, "May we call you by your first name?" and "Would it be OK with you if we asked a few questions about your emotions?"). We do our best to respect the patients' priorities, to respect their right to decide (with sufficient alternatives), *not* decide, to help with uncertainty (offering "don't know" and "don't understand" options, with explanations when appropriate), and to respect reluctance to respond.

Communication between patient and computer—and patient and doctor, as well, I would argue—should not be used to persuade the patient to answer questions the doctor deems important; rather, it should be used to outline the medical reasons for the questions so that patients can decide for themselves whether they care to answer. Patients should not have to answer questions against their will. In Wisconsin, we incorporated a "none of your damn business" option into the questions. We have since toned it down to "skip it," better accepted in Boston.

An expanded set of responses to yes-no questions enables patients to indicate uncertainty and lack of comprehension, to request clarification, and to bypass questions they don't care to answer. This reduces the number of uninformed responses and the coercion that can lead to inconsistency, subterfuge, and decreased validity. Most of our computer-based interviews also employ, to some extent, other mutually exclusive numbered choices, multiple choices with more than one response acceptable, and free-text responses.

In our experience, and the experience of most others who have studied dialogue between patient and computer, concern about the computer as a depersonalizing influence in dialogue with patients has been unfounded. Most patients who have had the opportunity "to talk to the computer" have found their experience to be pleasant, interesting, and informative.

The next step in our studies of patient-computer dialogue was to move beyond programs that take the medical history, which were designed primarily to collect information from the patient for use by the doctor. Our idea was to use the computer as a patient's assistant— to develop interactive computer programs that would help patients help themselves, as well as help their doctors.

AN UNEXPECTED DIETARY USE FOR THE COMPUTER

CHAPTER THREE

The Computer as a Patient's Assistant

Our early studies of dialogue between patient and computer were based on the premise that the computer interview could be valuable to the doctor for purposes of diagnosis and treatment. But I wanted to go further; I wanted to develop programs that would be valuable to the *patient* in diagnosis and treatment.

GUIDELINES FOR A PATIENT'S PROGRAM

My ideal interactive program for patients would have the following characteristics:

- *The program should be medically sound.* The authors' credentials—or better yet, experience—should be readily available for scrutiny.
- *The program should be easy to use.* It should be designed by people who understand the psychology of conversation with a computer, the human factors as well as the medical content. A few keystrokes or clicks of the mouse should be sufficient to gain access to the program, and moving from the opening words of welcome to the various options within the program should be a straightforward process. Ideally,

the program should be addressed to the literacy level of the user, and written in the user's native language.

• *The program should be truly interactive.* It should be easier for a person to obtain information from the computer than from a book. The program should be more than a page turner; the opposable thumb and forefinger are quite sufficient for this on their own, without benefit of electronics. The program should be capable of responding quickly to the wishes and needs of the individual user. It should also proffer appropriate and potentially useful alternatives that the person has not yet thought of. It should be able to ask questions with respect and thoughtfulness and answer questions in the same manner. When called upon to do so, the program should offer explanations, instructions, and suggestions. The user should be in charge.

• *The program should be of immediate benefit to the user.* The emphasis should be on the practical. Theoretical underpinnings and background information should be available to those who want to pursue them, but strategies for dealing with the situation at hand must be available first and foremost, at the top of the electronic menu, so to speak. A user might want to know the biochemistry of clotting blood, but not while dealing with a bleeding cut. Those of us in academia struggle to resist the temptation to begin all explanations with a discourse on the anatomy of the atom.

• *Confidentiality should be protected.* Only the individual user or persons whom the user has authorized should have access to the information obtained during the dialogue. The capability should exist, however, for pooling data from consenting users, who would remain anonymous, for use both in improving the program and in clinical research.

• *The computer should be fast and reliable.* In the event of problems, help should be on hand.

• *The program should be readily available.* People of all socioeconomic backgrounds should be able to use it in a place of convenience and at an affordable cost. Access to the computer should be as easy as access to the telephone.

• *The program should be subjected to formal study with volunteers in an experimental setting, before being offered to the public.* Results of the study, including helpfulness of the program and satisfaction of the volunteers, should be available to all who might subsequently want to use the program.

To my knowledge, no program yet exists that achieves this ideal. Certainly none of ours do. On the other hand, a number of people in the field are making progress, and I am optimistic.

—⌁⌁—

In our laboratory, Hollis Kowaloff, Alan Leviton, Douglas Porter, our colleagues, and I have studied the interactive computer as a patient's assistant in a variety of health-related areas.

HELPING WITH WHAT WE EAT

Food is on everybody's mind these days. We all have to eat and most of us would like to eat carefully but not to the point of compromising taste. Most of us know the three food groups (carbohydrates, proteins, and fats). Most of us know something about *essential* vitamins (those that must be included in our diets), and the *inessential* vitamins (those that we can synthesize from what we eat), and that there are also essential elements such as iron and calcium. Most of us know that chronic, excessive consumption of carbohydrates can lead to overweight, and that dietary fat can make us overweight and, particularly among men, more vulnerable to heart disease as we get older.

On the other hand, most of us will never be professional nutritionists, and we find ourselves these days confronted with a bewildering plethora of information in the press, often of a conflicting nature. It isn't just any fat that is bad for us, we read; saturated fat is the principal culprit. But knowing this we are still faced with questions such as which cooking oil to use (current wisdom favors olive oil) and which margarine to use in lieu of butter. Eating more calcium may be as important as eating less sodium to reduce blood pressure. Beta-carotene, once advocated as a vitamin supplement to help prevent cancer, has recently been declared ineffective. Caffeine keeps getting blamed as a causative substance for cancer of the pancreas— and then exonerated. It is pretty clear that a diet high in refined carbohydrates, such as the "simple" sugar sucrose, is a causative factor in dental cavities in children, but with fluoride in our drinking water, cavities have been reduced dramatically, independent of the amount of sugar we eat. Whether sugar is bad for us in other ways remains controversial.

In keeping with the state of confusion about nutrition and diet, and our interest in the computer as a patient's assistant, we asked ourselves whether an interactive program might help people alter their dietary behavior, when indicated, to their best possible nutritional advantage. This was really a rhetorical question; the answer in our minds was yes, and we set out to prove we were right. (There is no such person, at least in my experience, as a truly disinterested scientist.)

We set about to develop a dietary counseling interview in collaboration with Jelia Witschi of the Harvard School of Public Health, who became the mentor of the project. Writing in our programming language Converse (which we use for all our interviewing programs), we created a program that would ask questions dealing with general dietary behavior, elicit details of food intake on an average day, and plan with a person a weight-reducing diet of approximately 1500 kcal. During the interview, the program would offer dietary suggestions and, on completion, generate a printed summary for use by patients and nutritionists.

An Experiment

In a study with sixty-four volunteers (thirty-two men and thirty-two women), each with the self-diagnosis of simple overweight, the interview was found to assist the patients in organizing their thoughts about eating and in planning their own dietary behavior, and to assist the expert nutritionists who participated in the study, when volunteers and nutritionists subsequently met. In addition, the patients found their time with the computer to be a pleasant and personalizing experience.

Fifty-six of the sixty-four patients returned for the three-month visit, which was scheduled as part of the study. Of these, thirty-six (64 percent) had lost an average of seven pounds; seven (13 percent) had no weight change; and thirteen (23 percent) had gained an average of five pounds.

It was not our intention to suggest that the weight loss in this experiment should be attributed to use of the computer. All volunteers had sessions with a nutritionist as well as the computer. However, we are confident that the conversational computer can be helpful in studying the relative effectiveness of various approaches to dialogue with people who want to lose weight, and we are equally confident that the computer will prove to be a good medium for such dialogue when an effective approach is found.

The computer interview was especially good at helping people understand their own thoughts and actions. Various participants said, "It heightened awareness of eating habits"; "It gave me an almost exact picture of what I eat and drink daily"; and "The computer is yourself—you don't feel responsible to anyone except yourself."

Such comments suggest a personalizing effect that can be a particular advantage of the computer as an interviewer. Conversation with a computer is, after all, similar in some ways to conversation with oneself. Soliloquy can sometimes be helpful in promoting insight and, at least in this experiment, the computer was successful in enhancing self-awareness.

The computer was better at asking questions than at answering them. Volunteers could indicate when they didn't understand or were uncertain about their answers, but there was little opportunity for them to query the machine directly. Accordingly, the experiment gave us valuable insight about how we could make our programs more responsive to peoples' needs.

A revised and updated version of this program is currently in routine use by personnel at Beth Israel Hospital in Boston.

A PROGRAM FOR EMPLOYEE HEALTH

Beth Israel Hospital, a major teaching hospital of Harvard Medical School, has approximately five thousand employees. In 1985, the hospital implemented Johnson and Johnson's "Live for Life" program. This voluntary program, which was designed to promote physical and emotional well-being among the hospital's personnel, consisted of a self-administered (pencil-and-paper) health questionnaire, health education classes, and an exercise fitness center.

In 1990, in collaboration with clinicians at the hospital and members of the employee health department, we replaced the paper questionnaire with a computer-administered health screening interview for the hospital employees and staff clinicians. The interview is part of the integrated Center for Clinical Computing (CCC) clinical information system used throughout the hospital, and is available on any of over four thousand terminals. Conducted in private and with protection of confidentiality, the interview seeks information on medical problems and patterns of living for which behavioral change is considered desirable and offers advice and suggestions on matters of health and illness.

The Effect of Lifestyle

Like all our programs, the interview begins with words of welcome, information on how to proceed, and a brief discussion of the purpose of the program ("We hope we can help you discover how your lifestyle affects your health and what you can do to improve your health"). It assures the user that all responses will be kept in confidence and made available to clinicians only at the user's request.

Next there is a series of frames that teach the inexperienced user how to operate the computer terminal, how to change answers and back up to previous questions, and how to indicate uncertainty—by choosing "don't understand" or "maybe (don't know)"—and reluctance to respond—by choosing "skip it."

The interview itself begins with a section that elicits demographic information, with emphasis on the circumstances of each participant's employment at the hospital. The computer then lists the seven sections of the interview (General Medical History, Nutrition History, Exercise Patterns, Habits, Safety, Environment, and Stress) and offers participants the opportunity to select sections in order of their personal preference.

An optional component of the nutrition section is the twenty-four-hour recall, which begins by identifying the first meal or snack of the day and then asks about six potential eating periods. When the user has responded to all questions about a specific meal or snack, the program provides a chance to check the accuracy of the entries and list additional foods that come to mind. At the conclusion of the nutrition section, the user is asked to evaluate the accuracy and completeness of the entries and to indicate whether the meals or foods listed reflect typical eating patterns; if not, the program asks in what ways they are unusual. The twenty-four-hour recall may be repeated as often as desired.

As each section is completed, the program offers to display a summary of the information provided. With the nutrition section, the summary details the specific nutrients in each food eaten, with totals for each meal and total nutrient intake for the day plus a dietary evaluation showing actual and recommended nutrients.

At the end of the interview, the program offers a clinical evaluation of problems that could be favorably influenced by changes in behavior. In addition, the program offers information about referral services.

If, for example, a person mentions feeling depressed, the program provides the names and telephone numbers of places to turn to for help—the Employee Assistance Program, the Samaritans, and the hospital's emergency room.

Use of the Program

During a five-and-one-half-year period, 2,586 employees completed the interview. Each interview took about thirty minutes from start to finish. Most of the participants (97 percent) were between twenty and sixty years of age. About half of them classified themselves as "professional" (nurses are the largest group of employees), and the rest as "clerical or secretarial," "technical," "managerial," or "service" workers; 1 percent preferred not to answer this question.

During the course of the interview, 85 percent of the employees expressed an interest in the health-related programs offered by the hospital: 73 percent were interested in the fitness center, 38 percent in the stress-reduction program, 24 percent in the "management of your time" program, 12 percent in the low-back protection program, and 6 percent in the smoking-cessation program.

Forty-one percent of the participants who completed the interview availed themselves of the opportunity to visit the nurse for a follow-up evaluation and to consider entering one or more of the health-related programs. Fourteen percent answered yes to the question "Would you like to get more information about [safe sex practices] when you visit with the nurse?" Nine percent answered yes when asked "Do you have any questions about birth control?"—and most of these answered yes to the question "Would you like to talk about this when you visit with the nurse?" When participants communicated a desire to be contacted directly for further information and recommendations, this was forwarded to the nurse. With future versions of the program, we would like the computer program itself to be equipped to provide this information directly to those employees who would like it, on-line.

More than half the employees at the hospital who took the health screening interview also took the computerized twenty-four-hour dietary recall, and almost a third took it more than once. It was gratifying to learn from these people that the program was helping them to alter their diets in accordance with current nutritional wisdom as well as in a beneficial manner, from their personal perspective.

Real and potential difficulties in life were common among hospital personnel as indicated by the results of the interview: 57 percent of the respondents reported high levels of stress, and 43 percent reported feeling sad, discouraged, or hopeless in the previous month; 6 percent indicated that life sometimes did not seem worth living. (As soon as their responses were registered, these people were told by the computer where they could obtain help for their problems.) We hope these employees moved quickly to avail themselves of the opportunity offered by the computer.

As we have found with other computer-based interviews, the participants reacted favorably to this one: 85 percent responded positively when asked whether their time at the computer was worthwhile. The participants who indicated that they wanted to pursue health-related matters further were more likely to have found the interview worthwhile. The interview, it would seem, served to facilitate an interest in health and well-being.

When asked to compare the computer-based interview with an interview with a doctor or nurse, more participants indicated a preference for the computer. As in our earlier studies, however, the computer posed this question. Had a nurse or doctor asked the same question, the answer might have been different.

Sixteen percent of the participants answered yes to the question "Did the computer sometimes ask you more than you wanted to tell?" By contrast, 50 percent answered yes to the question "Did you sometimes want to tell the computer more than it asked?" Furthermore, participants were more likely to find the interview worthwhile if they were among those who wanted to tell the computer more than it asked. We interpreted these results as an indication that we were on the right track and that we should expand the program to make it more receptive and more informative.

These are difficult times for many people in this country, as reflected by the findings in our study. Personnel in hospitals and clinics, whose mission is to minister to the needs of others, often suffer undue physical and emotional hardships of their own, both at work and in their private lives. The health-promotion programs of the Beth Israel Hospital are offered to all hospital personnel, with the hope that they will become active participants in their care. And people are using the programs every day. We hope other hospitals will do what Beth Israel Hospital is doing to promote well-being among their own employees.

SELF-CARE

Urinary tract infection is a common and important medical problem among women, from adolescence through later life. By contrast, it is rare among men under the age of fifty. The anatomical reason for this disparity is the difference in the length of the urethra, the tube from the bladder through which urine is excreted. Being shorter in women, the urethra is less of a protective barrier to bacteria, which can find their way into the bladder, and, in a culture of residual urine, initiate a cystitis, or infection of the bladder. If the bacteria should then ascend to a kidney through one of the connecting ureters, a more serious kidney infection, or pyelonephritis, can result. In the great majority of cases, however, the infection remains in the bladder, an "uncomplicated urinary tract infection" that is readily cured, in most instances with one of the sulfa drugs.

Urinary tract infections treated in the traditional manner require individualized attention by a physician or nurse practitioner in a clinical setting—professional care that is inconvenient for the patient, sometimes unavailable, and always expensive. In the United States, urinary tract infections result in over six million visits to doctors' offices or other medical facilities each year. With a conservative estimate of $30 per visit, not including the cost of laboratory studies and medication, this is an annual expenditure of $180 million.

Consequently, my colleagues and I hypothesized that as an alternative, patient-computer dialogue could provide the basis for the diagnosis and treatment of urinary tract infections, in a manner at least as good as an office visit. We further hypothesized that this automated patient's assistant could be made available in the home, school, or workplace, in a manner substantially less expensive than traditional professional care.

The Patient's Assistant

In perhaps our most radical departure from the traditional, together with Howard Bleich, Linda Fisher, and Scott Johnson, we set about to test our hypothesis. In 1975, we developed a program designed to assist women in caring for themselves when suffering from an uncomplicated urinary tract infection. Integrated into the program were questions designed to make certain that the woman's infection was in fact uncomplicated; any indication of a more serious problem, for example, a history of fever that might indicate a kidney infection, would result in the recommendation that the patient seek further medical care from a physician. The program was designed for experimental trial in a clinical setting with close medical supervision by doctors and nurses. The long-range goal, however, was to have this program, if successful, modified for use by patients in their homes.

The Experimental Program

The program begins with words of welcome and a sequence of instructions about how to take the interview. The program then takes a history of the symptoms usually associated with a urinary tract infection ("If it is OK with you, we would now like to ask a few questions about urinary symptoms." followed by, "Are you bothered by pain or burning when you urinate?" "Are you urinating more often than you usually do?" and "Are you bothered by the unexpected, urgent need to urinate?").

The program then offers the patient instructions about providing a urine sample for analysis (to check for white blood cells, which might indicate an infection) and culture (to identify any bacteria that might be causing an infection). The interview is interrupted to allow the patient to provide a urine sample for laboratory studies. When the patient returns, the program resumes with medical questions dealing with urinary, gynecological, cardiological, gastrointestinal, and metabolic problems (for example, "Have you felt feverish within the past few days?" and "Have you ever been told by a doctor that you have high blood pressure?") to rule out complicating problems that would need care beyond the scope of the program. The program also tests the reliability of important questions by repeating them, and it resolves uncertainties that may arise, for example, when the patient does not understand a question. In the event of an abnormality or possible abnormality that might preclude continued participation, the medical logic incorporated into the program is used to construct words of advice and explanation and to suggest that the patient meet with a doctor.

If the program detects no reasons for referral, including no history of untoward experiences with sulfa, it proceeds to the therapy section, which presents six topics of possible concern about medication—effectiveness, cost, safety, dosage, route of administration, and "Can I get well without it?"—discusses these as they relate to treatment with sulfa, in the order of importance chosen by the patient—"You indicated that knowing how well sulfa works is perhaps most important to you. . . . Let's consider this first"—and offers opportunities to review information previously presented—"Before deciding about sulfa, would you like to go over anything again?"

Deciding for Yourself

Thereby informed, the patient is offered the choice of taking sulfa, taking nothing, considering another medicine, or indicating uncertainty. If the time to respond to this question is particularly long or short compared with a previous more neutral question (the program keeps track of response time automatically), the program mentions this and asks if the patient would like to reconsider her choice (short response times may indicate confident decision or uninformed consent; long response times may indicate thoughtful weighing of alternatives or considerable doubt).

As a further check for reliability, the patient is asked to indicate her decision at least twice. Patients who elect not to take sulfa are offered referral to a doctor. Those who elect to take sulfa are offered the option to start it immediately or to wait for the results of the culture. For those who elect to begin sulfa right away, the computer provides a suggested medication schedule. The program concludes with a series of questions about the patient's reaction to the interview—whether the program was helpful and whether she liked deciding for herself about taking the medicine.

The computer then prints out for the patient her medication schedule, a summary of the interview, a list of the signs of an adverse reaction to the sulfa, and a prescription to be filled in the pharmacy of her choice. The patient is then asked to call our laboratory at once if she is feeling worse or has reacted adversely to the sulfa, and to call in any event after three or four days to get the results of her culture and further advice.

Follow-Up

In the experimental sessions, a research assistant receives the follow-up telephone calls and enters the patient's responses to a detailed computer interview, which is read to the patient, at the computer terminal. With structured questions and suggestions presented by the computer, the assistant asks the patient whether her symptoms have disappeared, whether she has been able to take the medicine, and whether she has had any other problems.

Rules incorporated into the logic of the program guide the assistant in advising the patient over the phone and scheduling a return visit. If symptoms are persistent or there is evidence of a possible adverse reaction to the medication, the patient is advised to stop all medication and to return to the clinic as soon as possible. If the symptoms have abated, the patient is advised to return to the clinic in two weeks and, if she is willing, an appointment is scheduled. Patients who do not call within four days are contacted by the research assistant for the telephone interview.

A patient who returns for the follow-up visit is interviewed by the computer about urinary symptoms, whether she was able to take the medicine, and any problems that might have arisen. Then, after a brief review of instructions by the computer, she is asked to provide another urine sample for a repeat analysis and culture. If the interview or urinalysis indicates a persistent or recurrent infection, or if there are new symptoms that require attention, the patient is referred by the computer to a physician. In the event that the repeat urine culture demonstrates infecting bacteria, the patient is called and advised to return for further evaluation and treatment.

Putting the Program to the Test

In a preliminary clinical trial, the program performed to the satisfaction of the patients who participated and those of us who designed the study. Of forty-six patients who came to the clinic for help with their symptoms, which included pain with urination, ten were referred out of the program for consultation with a doctor, and thirty-six continued on to the therapy section of the interview. Among the thirty-six women who completed the program, "How well does the medicine work?" "Can I get well without it?" and "How safe is it?" were the most important considerations. Thirty-four of the patients decided to take the sulfa immediately, one patient decided to wait for the results of her culture (which turned out to be negative), and one was uncertain but eventually decided to take the sulfa.

Of the thirty-six patients who completed the interview, nineteen called our laboratory for their telephone interview, six were reached by one of us, and eleven could not be reached by telephone and were lost to the study. Of the twenty-five patients who were interviewed by telephone, twenty-four had taken at least some of their medicine, and the one who had not was about to start. Sixteen were asymptomatic and doing well, seven were feeling better, and two had not improved and were among those who were lost to further follow-up.

Fourteen of the patients returned to our laboratory for their follow-up visit. Eleven were asymptomatic and three still had symptoms. On repeat culture, two of the asymptomatic patients and the three symptomatic patients had persistent bacterial infections and were referred to a doctor for further care. The volunteers in this study were not billed for their visits.

The return rate among the volunteers was low—only fourteen of thirty-six patients (39 percent) returned for their second visit. On the other hand, this compares favorably with the return rate of all our patients with urinary tract infections, which is 25 to 30 percent.

Of the forty-two patients who were asked about their reaction to the initial interview (four of the ten who were referred to a doctor were inadvertently not asked these questions) forty found the computer "considerate," thirty-eight found the computer "thoughtful" and "respectful," and thirty-eight found their time at the computer well spent. When the thirty-six patients who continued into the treatment section were asked "How has it been to decide for yourself about sulfa, thirty found it to be "a good thing," three had "no preference either way," two were "not sure," and one thought it would be "better left up to someone else."

Upon leaving the session, patients spoke approvingly of their time with the computer: "No doctor has ever been as thorough with me as your machine" and "I hope you will have similar programs for other medical problems" were among the comments. And the majority of patients liked being able to make their own decisions about treatment.

This is consistent with all our findings on patient-computer dialogue. In our experience, concern about the computer as a depersonalizing influence in dialogue with patients has been unfounded. The interaction has been pleasant, interesting, informative, and empowering for the overwhelming majority of patients.

The Issue of Compliance

Physicians often complain that patients are noncompliant; they do not do what they are told. This resistance perplexes doctors. They can write prescriptions for patients, but they cannot control what patients do with the prescriptions.

I think it would be more appropriate to focus on the problem that may underlie noncompliance, the assumption that physicians are in charge of "their" patients and entitled to make decisions on their behalf. The very word *compliance* suggests submission to a higher authority.

I believe that patients who want to should be encouraged to make their own clinical decisions, as in our study of urinary tract infection, and that noncompliance should be regarded simply as disagreement with the doctor. Our data indicate that patients who elect to make their own medical decisions will be faithful to them, that they will do what they *tell themselves* to do. This has also been demonstrated by John Wennberg, Albert Mulley, and their colleagues when working with patients with diseases of the prostate gland. Furthermore, patients who make their own decisions will be responsible for the consequences of their choices, and their physicians will be spared the liability that accompanies medical paternalism. Self-reliant patients will be more realistic in their clinical expectations than patients who depend on their doctors' "orders." Subservient patients tend to regard their physicians as omniscient and are often incredulous when outcomes are unfavorable. This tendency may help explain why patients have been quick to sue and why doctors have fared poorly in court.

Goals for the Future

Urinary tract infection is a medical problem traditionally in the therapeutic province of the physician. Sulfa, the treatment of choice in most instances, requires a physician's prescription. In our study, all the computer-generated prescriptions were signed by one of the doctors. We hope this will be but a temporary expedient, however, required to conform with current regulations. I can think of no good reason why patients with uncomplicated urinary tract infection cannot prescribe for themselves, at least with the help of the computer. And the results of our study corroborate this judgment. If problems such as urinary tract infection can be managed in the home instead of the clinic, the cost savings will be substantial, and the quality of care can be at least as good, if not better. And more and more people are working to develop such programs. There is good work being done in a number of academic settings, including Case Western Reserve University, Dartmouth Medical School, Massachusetts General

Hospital, the Mayo Clinic, and the University of Wisconsin. The field is becoming active.

—⁓—

I used to dream of the interactive Benjamin Spock, a computer-based program in the home that would offer advice and suggestions about prevention of medical problems, as well as diagnosis and treatment when such problems arose. The idea was not to replace the doctor. The idea was to fill a void.

Now, with the increasing availability of the personal computer and the technology of nationwide and worldwide communication—the Internet and World Wide Web—this dream is beginning to be a reality. Every day new programs appear on disks for use on personal computers. We hope to get our programs into the home by means of the Internet, as well as with compact discs for the PC. But there are formidable barriers to overcome. Developing good interactive programs is difficult and expensive, and those of us in the field have a lot of work to do.

Let me turn now to studies of the computer in psychotherapy—a somewhat controversial field, to say the least.

"HE'S NOT MUCH TO LOOK AT, BUT HE'S A GREAT LISTENER, UNDERSTANDS MY DEEPEST NEEDS, AND DOESN'T GOLF."

CHAPTER FOUR

The Computer
in Psychotherapy

～～～ Since the early 1960s, the computer has been applied
with increasing frequency to the fields of psychology and psychiatry.
One of the first applications, at the Mayo Clinic, was to use the computer to score the results of the Minnesota Multiphasic Personality Inventory (MMPI), the most time-honored of diagnostic personality
tests. The inventory was administered manually but processed by computer, which was programmed to print descriptive phrases about the
patient's personality in addition to the numerical scores for use by
the psychologist. It turned out, however, that the early printouts
sounded pejorative. There were no favorable comments, even for patients with no emotional problems, and when patients had the chance
to read the reports, they objected. In Madison at the time, I began to
develop the Wisconsin Uniphasic Personality Inventory (WUPI),
which would say only positive things about a person. The WUPI was
never implemented, but personality tests, including the MMPI, are
much less critical of people than they used to be—all part of the patient power movement, I would contend.

Now it is common to have the computer actually administer the
personality test. Nicholas Covino, John Levine, our colleagues, and I

do this at Beth Israel Hospital as part of the hospital-wide Center for Clinical Computing (CCC) system; inventories for depression, anxiety, and problems with alcohol are all conducted by patient-computer dialogue, with a high degree of patient satisfaction.

The most common use of the computer in the clinical setting has been to collect information directly from the patient to help the psychologist and psychiatrist with both diagnosis and treatment. But the computer has also been used for psychotherapy, more commonly as an adjunct to the human therapist, but sometimes as a therapist on its own. Most computer-based psychotherapy has been done as research, in academic medical centers rather than in clinical settings. Computer-based psychotherapy is still in its infancy, but the future is bright, in my opinion.

Among the earliest ventures into psychotherapy, back in the 1960s, Joseph Weizenbaum, Kenneth Colby, and their colleagues wrote computer programs (Weizenbaum's was called Eliza after Shaw's heroine in *Pygmalion*) that took messages typed by the user, rephrased them with words of similar meaning, and responded in a manner suggestive of the nondirective psychotherapy first proposed by Carl Rogers.

Since then, a number of good programs have been developed and studied, and a wide variety of theoretical approaches have been employed. John Greist and his colleagues at the University of Wisconsin employed cognitive behavioral therapy in their program. First elucidated by Aaron Beck and his coworkers, cognitive therapy consists of three parts: the *didactic* component, in which the therapist explains the approach to be taken (for example in the treatment of depression); the *cognitive* component, in which the therapist elicits the patient's thoughts at the moment and helps the patient analyze the underlying maladaptive assumptions contributing to the depression; and the *behavioral* component, in which the therapist helps the patient schedule thoughts and activities to supplant the depression.

Written in Converse by Paulette Selmi, the Wisconsin program emulates the cognitive therapist. In a comparative study, the computer performed impressively—as well as the human therapist in reducing scores on tests of depression. Computer-based cognitive behavioral therapy has also been used with some reported success for patients with early Alzheimer's disease and stuttering problems.

VIRTUAL ENVIRONMENTS

Sometimes called "virtual reality," virtual environments date back to
World War II, when Edwin Link and Luis DeFlorez introduced the simulated airplane, which could be used for pilots in training without risk
to human or machine; most airlines now use computer-based virtual
cockpits for pilot training. But now, with the computer and miniature
components, the equipment for the virtual environment can be worn
on your head and hands as you move about, as shown on the movie
screen in Michael Crichton's *Disclosure*. Most of us have seen pictures
of the guy with the high-tech headset—replete with goggles, miniature
TV screens (with computer-based pictures of the simulated environment), and three-dimensional sound—and proprioceptive gloves that
send information about hand movements back to the computer in
charge. With the right equipment, you can move about in multiple environments while staying pretty much in place.

One of the most exciting applications of the virtual environment
has been its use in the treatment of phobia. By simulating the offend-
ing environment, the virtual environment enables the therapist to employ behavior therapy—habituating the patient by means of simulated
exposure. For example, Barbara Rothbaum and her colleagues at
Emory University in Atlanta have effectively treated acrophobia by
gradually exposing patients to greater and greater virtual heights in
the safety of the lab.

It is not my purpose, however, to review the psychotherapy programs of others, good as many of them are. That would be another
book. I would like now to discuss my own experience with the computer in psychology and psychiatry.

A PSYCHIATRY INTERVIEW

In 1968, Maxie Maultsby and I ventured into a field that was more
controversial than our other computer interviews at the time. We developed a computer-based psychiatric interview, designed as a general
review of behavioral problems, and introduced it to sixty-nine volunteers who had been scheduled for psychiatric evaluation. As with
other computer histories, the patients reacted favorably. They indicated a slight preference for the computer as an interviewer in comparison with the doctor. Some patients responded yes to preferring

the doctor *and* yes to preferring the computer, apparently not wanting to hurt the feelings of either and nicely demonstrating that human beings are not always Aristotelian in their logic. They also found the computer to be more thorough. And, once again, these patients were sometimes more comfortable with the computer than they were with the clinician while answering questions of a potentially embarrassing or emotionally painful nature.

The consensus among the nine participating psychotherapists was that routine computerized psychiatric histories, if available, would add a valuable dimension to their diagnostic evaluations.

Abreaction with the Computer

Among proponents of traditional psychotherapy, it is widely held that topics of major psychological importance are, at least sometimes, the most unpleasant and hence the most difficult to discuss. It is also believed that reluctance to discuss such difficult topics must be removed if therapy is to be effective. This tenet is held whether the reluctance is interpreted as resistance to *abreaction* (bringing emotionally laden topics from the unconscious to consciousness and open discussion), in accordance with the psychoanalytic concepts of Freud, or as resistance to *extinction* (the weakening of a conditioned response in the absence of reinforcing stimuli), in accordance with the behavioristic concepts of John Watson and B. F. Skinner. Furthermore, it is generally assumed that this resistance must be removed by means of the relationship established between patient and therapist.

There is evidence, however, that under some circumstances there is less resistance to such communication when it occurs in the absence of the human clinician, including the psychotherapist. This has been our experience. Patients have said that even when they were eager for their doctor to be informed, direct communication was sometimes difficult, and indirect communication by means of the computer was easier for them.

This phenomenon, which might be called abreaction with the computer, has been corroborated by others: in one study, patients undergoing treatment for alcoholism found it easier to report high levels of alcohol consumption to the computer than to a psychiatrist; in another, volunteers were more likely to reveal sexual problems to the computer than to a psychiatrist; and in a third, patients were more likely to communicate to the computer about a past criminal record, impotence, being fired from a job, and attempted suicide. And Steven Locke, our coworkers, and I have demonstrated that a computer-based screening interview could elicit more HIV-related factors in the health histories of potential blood donors than the standard questionnaire and interviewing methods currently in use at the Red Cross.

In each of those studies, however, the keyboard was the means of communication. What about talking aloud?

TALKING THERAPY

In 1971, I teamed up with my brother, Charles. We wanted people to be able to talk during a computer interview. Charles and I had the idea that the computer could facilitate talking therapy, that it could encourage people to talk out loud about matters of importance to them.

Talking Aloud Alone

Back in the late 1950s, in the Psychology Department at Harvard during that wild psychedelic era of Timothy Leary and friends, Charles had experimented with soliloquy. He had equipped a tape recorder with a device that emitted a repetitive click in response to sustained sound. It also tallied the number of clicks. Charles then employed teenage gang members from Cambridge to help him with his study. As long as the subjects in the experiment talked into the microphone, they could hear and see the counter adding up points at a steady rate, but whenever they stopped talking for more than a normal pause, the counter also ceased to give points. At the end of each experimental session of talk, each subject was paid according to the number of points accumulated during the session. The system worked well to initiate and maintain talk without a human listener in the room. Portions of the resulting tape recordings were indistinguishable from those of interpersonal interviews, and some of the participants said they felt better for having talked this way.

In the meantime, James Webb at Ohio University showed that people would talk alone when encouraged to do so by a standardized series of prerecorded (auditory) nondirective statements presented in a fixed sequence whenever there was a pause in the subject's speech. Expanding on this technique, Michael Dinoff and his colleagues at the University of Alabama promoted talk on the part of experimental subjects (including hospitalized patients) in response to fifteen requests from a prerecorded, videotaped interviewer who appeared on a screen whenever the person paused for two seconds. However, with this "talking alone" research, the stimuli promoting talk were presented in a predetermined sequence without branching; no use was made during the interviews of information provided by the person. In most clinical situations, by contrast, information obtained from the patient is used in subsequent conversation.

Speech-Understanding Systems

In the context of this discussion, it is important to keep in mind that computer-based speech-understanding systems are complex, expensive, limited in capabilities, and not yet readily available except in rudimentary form. Charles and I had the idea that the computer did not have to *understand* what was being said (and still doesn't) to help people help themselves. In other words, the computer could facilitate beneficial soliloquy.

The Talking Cure

Talking therapy, or the "talking cure," as Anna O. first called it in 1881, has a respected place in Western medicine. Ever since the first century A.D., when the Roman physician Celsus recommended the doctor-patient relationship as a treatment for depression and mania, dialogue between doctor and patient has had a major role in psychotherapy. Although there are important theoretical and practical differences between the various schools of talking therapy, all hold to the premise that the presence of the therapist and the relationship that results are essential to the therapeutic process.

There are problems with talking therapy as traditionally practiced, however. Typically, many sessions are required for treatment; few patients can afford the cost, and third-party payers—particularly those in the business of managed care—are reluctant to commit themselves to financing long-term therapy. Furthermore, hard-to-control variables, so important to the art of human discourse, lend uncertainty to scientific study and to our knowledge of how or whether desired goals are achieved through clinical conversation. Standards of comparison for controlled studies are difficult to establish. Therapists, even within the same school of thought, differ from each other and are themselves inconsistent. And the interested therapist, motivated to corroborate clinical judgment and theoretical doctrine, may bring bias to the session, unwittingly communicated by verbal and nonverbal cues, and thus evoke responses that conform to expectations.

COMPUTER-ASSISTED SOLILOQUY

The computer is more easily subjected to the rigors of scientific investigation than the traditional dialogue between therapist and patient. Charles and I had three hypotheses: that the presence of a therapist is not essential in talking therapy, because patients will talk aloud alone about matters of psychological importance; that speaking out, as opposed to thinking quietly, is important to the effectiveness of psychotherapy; and that the doctor-patient relationship, although often beneficial, can sometimes inhibit frank disclosure. In the latter case, soliloquy can be more effective than dialogue with a therapist.

We reasoned that text on a computer screen could be a good stimulus for talk and that keyboard responses could be used to select text that would encourage talk about subjects of relevance to the person. Accordingly, we developed a computer program capable of controlling a tape recorder (and sensing when someone was talking into it) in conjunction with conducting a medical interview. With this program, people could be encouraged to talk about their own problems, and recorded messages could be left for the doctor.

We used a PDP-12 computer (Digital Equipment's successor to the LINC) connected electronically to the control unit and microphone of a tape recorder. This was old-fashioned technology by today's standards, but it worked well for our purposes at the time. The user's responses determined the questions presented next. The time elapsed after the display of a question and intervals between points of reference in the interview could also be used as conditions for proceeding or not proceeding.

The occurrence of sound (as sensed at the microphone) was relayed to the computer and was available as another contingency for presenting new text on the screen. There was *no* comprehension by the program of what was actually said. The computer could only detect the presence or absence of sound. However, information obtained by keyboard responses during the course of the interview could be used as the basis for encouraging the user to talk, and the event of talk (or lack of it) could be used to determine what would subsequently appear on the screen. The tape recorder was under computer control and could be turned on whenever speech was being encouraged. Recordings of all discussion with the computer were thus available to us for transcription and analysis.

The Interview

The interview, which was initially designed for men, opened with words of welcome and instructions telling how to interact with the computer. These were followed by a series of medical-history questions dealing with common emotional problems beginning with sadness ("Have you been feeling sad or down in the dumps?"). If the answer was yes, the respondent was told that he would have an opportunity to discuss this sadness later on if he wished. The program then asked about the loss of someone close, loneliness, social or marital problems, problems with parents, problems at school, difficulty with self-expression, problems of a sexual nature, problems with drugs, and insomnia.

After the medical-history questions, the computer asked if the user was willing to discuss his sadness ("You indicated that you have been feeling sad; are you willing to talk a bit about this?") or whichever of the problems, if any, was detected in the interview. If so, the tape recorder was turned on automatically, and the program presented a statement encouraging talk about the problem. If the user delayed, he was asked if he was having trouble getting started, and if so, he was given advice on how to begin. The user responded to most questions by means of the keyboard; when he spoke, he did so into the microphone located between the screen and the keyboard.

As soon as talk was sensed by the computer, the program branched to a statement that acknowledged and encouraged the discussion. If the user paused without indicating that he wanted to stop, the program asked him to tell what he thought was most responsible for the problem and later what, in his opinion, would be most helpful. Next, the computer presented statements that encouraged discussion about personal feelings at the moment; something about the respondent that could not possibly be true; a personal problem considered in a very rational way; and an example of behavior that, in the respondent's opinion, was a "responsible act"—topics considered important to the psychology of Carl Rogers, Freud, Albert Ellis and Maxie Maultsby, and William Glasser. Discussion was acknowledged with words such as "We are 'listening' to you talk about. . . . If finished, press 'GO.'" Once again, delays in getting started and prolonged pauses during discussion resulted in explanation and encouragement. A person could refuse to discuss anything suggested by the computer and could leave a topic at any time.

An Experimental Trial

Thirty-two men between the ages of eighteen and twenty-six (none of whom were currently receiving psychotherapy) were recruited through colleges and medical schools in the Boston area and paid to participate in the experiment. Each subject was interviewed by one of us, as well as by the computer, half interacting first with the computer, and half first with one of us. We attempted to follow basically the same protocol as the one followed by the computer, and our interviews were also recorded on tape. Inadvertently, the question concerning the loss of someone close was omitted from our (human) questioning. In each setting discussion of a problem detected by history was limited to ten minutes, and discussion of each of the topics relating to the schools of psychotherapy was limited to five minutes.

The volunteers came to our laboratory three times: for an orientation session, at which the design of the experiment was explained with emphasis on the fact that the computer would not understand what was being said and recorded; for the experimental interviews; and for an evaluation session when each subject was asked, by written questionnaire, a series of questions regarding his reaction to the interviews. Each subject then met with us for an informal consideration of the experiment. All the participants gave express permission to use their recordings for analysis, demonstration, and publication, with the understanding that we would protect their confidentiality. Analysis of the content of what was said was performed by three independent observers using the "Experiencing Dimension" developed by Eugene Gendlin.

Responses to the Interviews

All thirty-two participants had something to say to the computer as well as to the doctor, and many talked in poignant ways about aspects of their lives. Life had not been easy for most of them. One subject discussed a problem with a girlfriend as follows:

My girlfriend is emotionally unstable. She has problems with herself. She doesn't seem to be able to figure out why she's so frustrated. She has anxiety attacks. For that reason, she gets cold, frustrated, and angry over things that most people wouldn't normally get angry and frustrated about. Sometimes I think the way she feels is rubbing off on me. Sometimes I'm afraid to get too close to her for fear of my own sanity if I ever left her, or for fear of her own sanity if I ever left her. Sometimes I think I would like to wind the whole situation down and bring it to a halt. I don't know whether I stay in it because of myself or because of her. There is more, but I wouldn't want to stall any longer. [Here there was a prolonged pause followed by encouragement from the computer to discuss possible causes of the problem.] Her anxiety attacks . . . and being unable to be sure whether I can handle them or not. She goes to see a social worker, and she tells everything to the social worker, and I think she almost feels that she can't tell the problems to me because she has this thing with the social worker being her dominant person—someone she can look up to and trust—whereas she feels she might be in some sort of competitive relationship with me, and she doesn't want to lose me. Therefore sometimes—oh, a lot of times—she's afraid to even talk to me. We have a communication breakdown and it's very frustrating . . . I just feel that it's a great emotional strain on me . . . whereas I'm working five hours for four nights and going to school full time . . . I love the girl but I don't know whether I can handle it. [In this instance, the computer interview preceded the doctor interview.]

Emotional problems were common among the volunteers; only three of the thirty-two answered no to all the medical history questions. Of the twenty-nine people who had one or more problems as elicited by the computer or by one of the doctors, twenty-two discussed a problem with both the computer and the doctor. Twelve of these talked about their feelings of sadness, and ten discussed other problems.

Five of the participants discussed a problem only with the doctor. With two of these people, questions that had been answered negatively to the computer were answered positively to the doctor and the problems were discussed only with him. A third person did not care to talk with the computer about a sexual problem that he had already discussed with the doctor. The other two, each of whom had first established good rapport with a doctor, expressed hostility to the computer while talking to it. Later, they told us they could have communicated better with the machine if they had not seen the doctor first. The following are two excerpts from one discussion:

> Personal feelings right now are . . . I certainly do have something that might be interesting to talk to a doctor about. It just seems very impersonal to be speaking to a machine that really shows—doesn't show any emotion or . . . I don't have anything to say to this monster here!
>
> I suppose I could do something for somebody else in the future by maybe saying something about this computer. It just doesn't seem to relax you enough or make you feel warm enough . . . If there is anything personal or something that is bothering you, it's hard for a person like myself to speak to a machine that's flashing green and black . . . sorry!

Two other people, whose single problem was the loss of someone close—the problem inadvertently neglected by the doctors—discussed it only with the computer.

The topics from the four schools of psychotherapy proved to be good promoters of talk for the computer, as well as for the doctors. In response to the request by the computer to discuss a personal problem in a very rational way (in accordance with the school of Ellis and Maultsby), one person said the following:

> Well . . . I'm having trouble finding out who I am . . . but I also have to take in all sides of the thing. I have to figure out what it is that makes me up . . . what differences I have from other people . . . what ways I can do things better, or not as good. I have to take into account my intellect . . . my personality . . . how I do things . . . how it affects other people . . . how I actually relate to other people. I look at it all, and you have to sit back and look at it rather objectively. You have to so detach yourself from it to see who you are and how you are relating to these other people. Ah . . . I think I do take the time to sort of look at things objectively. I can sort of remove myself actually from the . . . situation and look at it as if I were looking at another character . . . or at least I think I can.

Eight people indicated by the questionnaire and subsequent discussion that they felt more at ease while talking to the computer than while talking to the doctor. One person, when asked by the computer to discuss his personal feelings at the moment (in accordance with Carl Rogers), said the following:

> Ah . . . at present I feel sort of strange. This is the first time I've ever talked to a computer or used a computer . . . Um . . . I . . . well, as far as how I understand the experiment, the primary objectives of this experiment are . . . I'll tell you my feelings talking into a computer. From what I understand . . . the experiment is to compare one's response to a series of questions asked by a computer and a series of questions asked by a doctor. At the moment I feel like I'm talking into a tape recorder. I'm not really nervous . . . I have no qualms about talking into the recorder or into the computer. I . . . well, at the time I . . . it's something useful . . . I feel these things are going to be observed by humans, by doctors, so I feel no qualms about talking into this. In a way I think I rather like talking to a computer. There's nobody to bother me . . . I can say whatever I feel like and there's nobody looking to respond to what I say. It's sort of an indifference that is . . . that is here, and it has no effect on the way I talk as far as if you say something and somebody responds in a negative manner, you tend to shy away from continuing in that line. Well, there is none of that in talking to a computer . . . so I feel OK in talking to him [sic].

Variability of the Interviewer

One problem fundamental to research on the psychology of interviewing is the variability of the human interviewer. The same doctor may react differently to different people or at different times of the day and, by varying his or her interviewing technique, alter the way in which people respond to the questions. With the computer, the interviewing stimuli are consistent from person to person, and variations between people are more likely to be due to their actual differences than to the interviewing technique of the computer.

Likewise, in a study that compares people's responses over time, if the individuals are consistent in their responses to the computer interviewer and more varied in their responses to the doctors, this would indicate that the variability was due to changes developing in the doctors' technique rather than to changes in the people being interviewed. In this study, the participants were more revealing if they spoke to the doctors in the morning rather than in the afternoon, whereas they were equally revealing to the computer in the morning and afternoon. The absence of diurnal variability in computer sessions supports the interpretation that the doctors, rather than the subjects, were responsible for this difference and were perhaps poorer interviewers in the afternoon.

Furthermore, in the morning, when revelation in speech with the doctors was more substantive overall, it was more substantive still if the doctor interview came before the computer interview. In the afternoon sessions, however, there was more substantive revelation to the doctors among those whose computer sessions came first.

It is possible, therefore, that even in a traditional clinical setting, patient-computer dialogue could facilitate subsequent dialogue with a therapist, particularly if the therapist is in a relatively uncommunicative phase of his or her daily cycle.

Reactions to the Experiment

As judged by responses on the written questionnaire, the participants had varied reactions to the experiment and differed widely in their comparisons of the methods of interviewing. In general, reactions were more favorable to the human interviewers than to the computer. As designers of the experiment, Charles and I were naturally eager to have the computer do well as an interviewer. But the bias was at least in part balanced by our perceptions of ourselves as good interviewers—and perhaps even by a bit of sibling rivalry.

The attitudes of participants regarding the two interviewing situations were influenced by differences between doctors and by time of day and sequence of sessions. In general, Dr. A elicited more favorable reactions from participants in his afternoon sessions, Dr. B from those in his morning sessions. Overall, the participants seemed to relate somewhat better to Dr. A (we are not telling who is who).

Criticisms from the volunteers were helpful as we planned revisions in the program. Twenty of the thirty-two felt pressed for time while talking to the computer, and twelve indicated that they would have liked more time to talk to the machine. Accordingly, we adjusted the timing in subsequent programs in an effort to eliminate unnecessary interruptions and to put more patience into the system.

Some Thoughts About This Study

The computer in this experiment, though noncomprehending as a listener, was informed as an interviewer. It used information acquired by history questions to promote conversation appropriate to the person. When programmed to ask specific questions about what the person has just been saying, the computer can gain information about the content and use this in prompting subsequent discussion.

The study demonstrated that people will talk to a computer about problems of importance to them and about subjects of importance to psychologists and psychiatrists, and will sometimes do so in the same way they talk to a doctor. Four of the participants thought they might have been helped by talking to the computer, and eight believed that the solitude in which they talked to the computer actually helped them verbalize their thoughts. Those who saw the computer first seemed to have an easier time talking to it than those who saw a doctor first. Perhaps the process of being referred from man to machine evoked feelings of rejection. The study did not directly address the issue of therapeutic effectiveness, however.

COMPUTER-ASSISTED SOLILOQUY IN A STUDY OF ANXIETY

In a more recent experiment, one designed to study the effectiveness of soliloquy with a specific emotional problem, we programmed a computer to conduct an automated interview that would address the symptoms of anxiety. In doing so, we did our best to incorporate improvements into the interview on the basis of our experience with earlier programs.

Once again the computer communicated in text on the screen, and the user responded at the keyboard and via a microphone beneath the screen. Again, the computer was oblivious to the meaning of spoken words, and the user was so informed. On the other hand, the machine could respond to the occurrence of speech at the microphone, to the durations of speech and silence, to the time elapsed between various points of reference in the interview, to entries on the keyboard, and to the time the user took to respond, and it could use these factors to direct the course of the interview. In addition, the user's heart was being monitored with wire leads connected to a cardiotachometer, which transmitted the user's heart rate to the computer.

The interview began with words of welcome ("Hello there! Please find the <Go> key on the keyboard and press it."), followed by instructions about use of the keyboard ("The <Go> key is on the far right of the keyboard. Press it if you can."), acknowledgment and encouragement ("Exactly! Try it again."), instructions on the use of the microphone ("When the computer detects the sound of your voice at the phone, it will respond with some acknowledgment, like 'listening.' Try saying a few words."), and a request for the user's first name and for permission to use it during the interview. As a measure of anxiety at the beginning of the interview, the introductory section concluded with the Spielberger State anxiety measure, which consists of twenty questions designed to assess a person's level of anxiety at the moment.

The computer then proceeded to the section on anxiety. Introductory comments ("Most people are nervous, tense, or anxious, at least sometimes.") were followed by questions about the occurrence of anxiety when alone, with friends, with strangers, in a crowd, at a party, at school (if the user was a student), at work, and at home. Along the way, the computer encouraged the user to talk aloud about feelings ("Now tell yourself how you feel when you are anxious. Speak out loud, into the phone.") and about each of the situations in which they had occurred. Next, the computer encouraged the user to try to become anxious. ("Make a mental list of the circumstances most likely to make you anxious . . . now list them to yourself out loud.") The section concluded with a repeat presentation of the State anxiety measure.

The computer then turned to the subject of relaxation. ("You have talked about being anxious . . . now the idea is to dwell on a more comfortable state . . . relaxation.") The computer asked about the user's ability to relax under the circumstances that had been discussed in the section on anxiety, and then encouraged talking aloud about relaxation. ("Talk a bit about being at ease with strangers . . . say a little more if you can.") Then it encouraged the user to talk aloud about circumstances most conducive to relaxation and experiences with relaxation (as opposed to anxiety), and to develop and discuss strategies for relaxation in the future. The interview ended with a repeat of the State anxiety measure, a request for suggestions about the program, and thanks.

As a control for purposes of experimental comparison, we developed a "thinking interview" that encouraged the user to think quietly, as indicated by pressing a button instead of talking aloud. Otherwise, the wording and manner of presentation were identical in the two interviews. A control interview of this quality—identical in all respects except the variable being studied—is rare in studies of interviewing and was a principal strength of this experiment.

Experimental Trial

Forty-two men between the ages of twenty and thirty (none of whom were currently receiving psychotherapy) were recruited through colleges and graduate schools in the Boston area and paid to participate in the study. During preliminary sessions, the volunteers were divided into two matched groups—the talking group and the thinking group— on the basis of comparable scores on the computer-administered State anxiety and Taylor Manifest Anxiety measures and on the basis of comparable past experience with computers. At the end of the session, each volunteer was asked, by written questionnaire, about his reaction to the interviews.

Results

The two measures of anxiety improved in the experimental group but not in the control group. Both the mean heart rate and the State anxiety scores of the twenty-one volunteers in the talking group went down significantly between the beginning and the end of the interview. In the thinking group, by contrast, the drop in scores and heart rate was not statistically significant. Furthermore, the talking group spent more time talking aloud than the thinking group spent thinking quietly. During the relaxation section of the talking interview, the time devoted to talking was found to correlate significantly with both the drop in anxiety scores and the drop in heart rate—the more time spent talking, the greater the change. During the relaxation section of the thinking interview, by contrast, there was no significant correlation between the time devoted to thinking and changes in anxiety scores and heart rate. As judged by responses on the written questionnaire, the participants reacted favorably to the experiment in general, being equally well disposed to both the talking and the thinking interviews.

Implications

The primary approach with the soliloquy interview—to encourage each subject to speak first about anxiety, then about relaxation, and finally about personally developed strategies for replacing anxiety with relaxation—appears to have been effective under the experimental circumstances of this study. Encouragement to talk about relaxation was more effective than encouragement to think about it, as judged by the time devoted to each and the reductions in heart rate and State anxiety scores in the talking group. The correlations between these reductions and the time devoted to talking aloud indicate that computer-assisted soliloquy was more beneficial than thinking quietly in promoting relaxation. It would seem that talking aloud helps to keep us on track—on mental course, so to speak—when we are developing strategies that could promote our mental health.

The participants in this study were not patients; they were paid volunteers whose mean State anxiety scores at the start of the study were substantially lower than they would have been among men with the clinical diagnosis of anxiety. It is possible that computer-assisted soliloquy would have produced more striking results among patients with the symptoms of anxiety.

With the computer in our research, the variability and bias of the human interviewer can be eliminated as independent variables, and standards for comparison, such as the thinking interview for comparison with the soliloquy interview, can be more readily established. In the future, we plan to use the computer to study soliloquy further, both as an independent approach to therapy and as an adjunct to more traditional methods.

Paying our volunteers (a reversal of the usual arrangement between psychotherapist and client) did not seem to impede discussion. In fact, our subjects behaved very much like patients when discussing their problems. Still, people who come for help may react differently to the computer. There is much uncertainty these days about the effectiveness of any of the existing approaches to talking therapy, and it is not easy to evaluate the computer. But in spite of uncertainty about what works and what does not, psychotherapists are in demand and are often unavailable; where they are available, they are expensive. If the computer can help, and we believe it can, many people stand to benefit.

Abreaction with Computer-Assisted Soliloquy

In our first study of computer-assisted soliloquy, eight of the thirty-two volunteers indicated that "it might be easier to confess some things to the computer than to the doctor," whereas nineteen indicated "it might be easier to confess some things to the doctor." In the experiment with the anxiety program, twenty-four of the forty-two volunteers indicated that it "might be easier to talk to a computer about some things," whereas eighteen indicated it "might be easier to talk to a doctor." These responses indicate that under some circumstances, people also feel less resistance when talking about emotionally laden problems in the absence of a therapist.

Soliloquy in Everyday Life

In informal surveys, most of the people we ask indicate that they talk aloud alone, at least on some occasions. Charles and I believe that talking alone is practiced sporadically by almost everybody in our culture, even in the absence of a computer or other experimental devices. On the other hand, it is practiced systematically by almost no one. Yet when we encourage people to talk aloud alone on their own, systematically when possible, they tell us they feel better for doing so.

The fact that some mental patients talk to themselves (to their benefit, in our view) does not mean that if you do, you will become a mental patient. Quite the opposite. You may find that it helps reduce emotional tensions by providing an outlet, for example, for hostility. Contrary to the common notion that soliloquy is a manifestation of mental illness, we believe that it is normal behavior—behavior that serves to help maintain emotional equilibrium. Because of its link with mental illness, however, soliloquy is not socially acceptable; to be overheard talking alone can be cause for embarrassment. Even we don't recommend talking to yourself in front of others; we wouldn't think it was crazy, but they might. The trick is to get off where nobody can hear you, and then let loose.

Soliloquy therapy is probably the world's smallest school of psychotherapy, to date. There is reason, however, to believe that the number of adherents to the school will grow. We hope that as a result of our studies with the computer, people will be more comfortable with soliloquy—theirs as well as others'. There is little restriction on the number of people who can try it and little reason to doubt its safety. And as Groucho Marx said in assessing "free love," at least the price is right.

ARE THEY TALKING TO SOMEONE?

Remarks made to a computer, in our experience, are not readily distinguished from those made to persons, even when emotional problems are at issue. The following selections from our experimental interviews—all from volunteers who gave permission to publish their remarks—contain no obvious references to the computer or the doctor. Can you tell which were told to him and which to it? (You'll find the answers at the end of this chapter.)

1. Well, my sadness primarily stems from the fact that I see so many things going on around in society, in the world, but the things that I find hard to accept and I guess that I'm somewhat of an idealist. I see things that should not be. You know when you stop and consider that civilization in various forms has been going on for the past ten thousand years, it seems rather disheartening to look around you and see that man really has not progressed. Technology has progressed but the wars are the same.

2. I generally try to stay away from sex . . . ah . . . with women because it's usually too much of a hassle after everything is said and done to be worth the while of going out and having sex with women.

I don't know how to really express it in more detail having been caught short without having thought about what I would say. I think I generally don't receive enough spiritual compensation to make up for the spiritual effort in any kind of a relationship with women. It's pretty impossible for me now to have any kind of meaningful sexual relationship with women.

3. I could never be a good musician. I have no sense of rhythm. That bothers me.

4. Well, at this moment I feel pretty well at ease although a little confused about the procedure here. I don't know, I'm a pretty well-adjusted person. Things don't tend to bother me unless they're very important to me and right now I'm in a fairly secure situation and I feel pretty well at ease. There isn't anything that's bothering me right now. I think the only feeling, the only word that could express my feelings right now is one of contentment at what I'm doing.

5. I feel that I am in a stage in my life where I am coming to understand myself and part of this is to understand my sexual role and I'm changing mentally so, as I mature more I have to understand who I am going to be and I'm trying to adjust to who I am as I'm becoming

who I will be. It's just a general problem actually, knowing who I am at the moment and ah, it's not altogether serious. I realize what I'm doing and ah, I have a pretty good hold on myself. It's just that it is a big problem understanding yourself and your sexuality.

6.   Well, recently I lost my grandfather who I was fairly close to. I'm really willing to answer any specific questions. I don't know exactly what to say. I've been closer to other people than that, but my grandfather is the closest person to me that had died. Um . . . I was prepared for his death in that he had been sick for an extensive period of time, so that, ah, his death was more of a blessing than anything else in that it ended his suffering and hopefully he is having his heavenly reward if there be one. Um . . . I guess that's really all I have to say about it, since there are no specific questions."

7.   Well, I suppose I'll begin with—my vocabulary isn't that good—my amount of words isn't that hot and ah, I can express myself when I'm writing and I get the point across, but when I'm talking I seem to mumble and stutter so ah, that's the problem.

8.   [Pause.] Yeah, I have trouble expressing myself, all right. I can express myself when I'm writing, but I can't seem to do it when I'm talking; I have a little trouble. I have a limited vocabulary. I seem to stutter every time I begin to talk and that will be my problem of expressing myself.

In spite of good research with the computer as psychotherapist, it is still unusual for human therapists to employ computing in clinical practice. Before such programs become widespread in their use, they should follow the guidelines of any good computer-based patient's assistant—they should be medically sound; they should be easy to use; they should be truly interactive; they should be of immediate and if possible long-range benefit to the patient; they should protect confidentiality; they should be fast and reliable; they should be readily available to people of all socioeconomic backgrounds; and they should be studied for safety and effectiveness. We will continue with our efforts in this direction.

Turn with me now to a technological revolution that is bringing computing to patients everywhere.

—–⁓—

Answers to the who's-talking-to-whom quiz:

1. Computer
2. Doctor
3. Doctor
4. Computer
5. Computer
6. Computer
7. Doctor
8. Computer

CHAPTER FIVE

The Patient On-Line

Until 1980, patients had little direct access to computing. Patient-computer dialogue was for the most part limited to research projects in academic institutions that could afford computing facilities. Computing outside of medical centers was talked about, but in futuristic parlance. As for computing in the home, this was but a dream for some and a pipe dream for others. There were of course, television games in the 1970s that employed computer technology, but they were toys. There was also the original handheld calculator, the Pocketronic, which was available in 1970 for $400, but this was not considered a real computer. Some visionaries, such as Ken Olsen, the founder of Digital Equipment Corporation and a pioneer in the development of real-time, interactive computers, took it for granted that computers would be used in the home, but as recently as the late 1970s, it was common wisdom that computers would be impractical as domestic machines.

What most of us did not foresee was the personal computer, which would change our way of thinking forever. Expensive at first and with limited use—interactive games and spreadsheet accounting were staple fare—it caught on rapidly during the 1980s. The first major breakthrough in personal computing software was the word processor, which replaced the typewriter almost as quickly as the calculator replaced the slide rule (calculators were selling for $3 last time I checked). With rapidly advancing technology in its microprocessors and other inner workings, and with remarkable developments in magnetic disk storage, the PC has carried us into a vast new electronic era. The machines are getting more powerful, more portable, and less expensive as I write. It is estimated that there are some forty million PCs in the United States alone.

The amount of information available to us on disk is growing daily, and medicine on disk is keeping pace. There is more for the doctor than the patient, thus far, but the patient is catching up, with programs that promise sage advice and offer home remedies for a variety of ailments. It's hard to keep up. Some disks are free, some are reasonably priced, and some are expensive. Some are good, some are not so good, and some are bad. It's hard to judge. I try to keep in mind my eight guidelines for judging a program, but too often there is little or no information accompanying the disk to tell us how often people use the program, how much they like it, and how well it works. But I do not mean to demean this powerful technology, which is dear to my heart. Programs such as these, if well written and well tested, hold great promise for helping people help themselves with matters of health and disease. Furthermore, a Medical House Call on disk would be substantially less expensive these days than a house call in person. One important solution to the rising cost of medical care is enlightened self-care in the home. And for good or for bad, patient-computer dialogue is in the home to stay.

It has been said, however, that the only thing constant about computing is that it changes. Consistent with this idea, there is a new technology across the land that at once greatly expands the number of programs available on our personal computers *and* enables us to interact with others. This is computer-based telecommunication.

TELECOMMUNICATION

The first computer-based telecommunication system in the United States was established in the late 1960s by the Department of Defense. The purpose was to enable workers in defense facilities to send information from facility to facility as well as to industrial centers and academic institutions involved in military projects. As the program evolved, a large network of intercommunicating computers was formed—ARPANET (Advanced Research Projects Agency Network)—that permitted nationwide electronic communication among those who were engaged in defense activities. At the heart of the network was a standardized protocol for electronic communication—TCP/IP (Transmission Control Protocol/Internet Protocol), which still exists today. TCP/IP is the process whereby packets of information are transmitted from one computer to another, passing en route through multiple intermediary computers and computer networks by what has been called a series of hand-shaking procedures.

The original purpose of ARPANET was to provide a means of sending large files of information from one computer center to another, and this proved to be a powerful form of telecommunication. Within a decade, the uses for interinstitutional communication, real and potential, had extended far beyond the ambit of any military objectives.

In the early 1980s, the National Science Foundation (NSF) replaced the Department of Defense as the principal source of government funding for this rapidly growing system. With ARPANET as the electronic framework, the NSF sponsored the development of a nationwide network, now called the Internet, or Net for short, that would link smaller networks of computers in government departments, state as well as federal, together with industrial and academic research centers; and the NSF offered grants to support colleges and universities in their effort to get their own computers and link them to the network. It was not long before the individual user without institutional affiliation could also gain access, if equipped with a personal computer, TCP communication software, modem, and telephone line. Most colleges and universities in the United States now offer free access to the Internet for students and faculty alike, and there is progress toward access in our secondary schools as well.

As I write, the Internet is a telecommunications system that connects about twenty thousand smaller networks of computers that in turn serve computers in multiple government, industrial, and academic agencies overseas as well as in the United States. There are also about fifteen million private citizens with access to the Internet. Current estimates are that close to forty million people have passwords, and the number is growing rapidly. In the meantime, NSF support is being replaced by funding from private companies that market access to the system on a regional basis. Now anyone with the necessary equipment can sign on with a local telephone call and use the Internet at a rate as low as $15 per month. Soon the Internet should be self-supporting, without funds from the government.

The Internet is loosely managed by members of the Internet Society, volunteers from among those who develop, enhance, and maintain the network. Criticized in years gone by as a closed-minded group of computerniks, the society now eschews high-tech elitism and works toward the goal of open access. Members of the Internet Society may differ on technical issues, but they share a common commitment to democratic principles.

The World Wide Web

Users worldwide have put information on the Internet for others as well as themselves. The File Transfer Program (FTP), one of the most powerful technical capabilities of the Internet, permits transfer of files from one computer to another at the beck and call of any user. Accordingly, many thousands of data repositories on a wide range of topics are available to each and every person who signs on to the Internet. The list of subjects, from aardvark to Zulu, and in medicine, from abdomen to zygote, is encyclopedic in scope. On the other hand, when you are looking for information of specific relevance to your interests at the moment, the logistics of searching can be a formidable, often bewildering, task. Raw access to the Internet is not friendly.

It is common in computing for easy-to-use programs to be needed to help with difficult ones, and a number of programs have been developed to ease access to the Internet. Telnet, for example, lets your computer connect to one of the computers on the Internet and behave as if it were a terminal; Gopher, developed at the University of Minnesota and named after the university mascot, offers access to resources on the Internet by a series of menus; and Veronica (very easy rodent-oriented netwide index to computerized archives) indexes the Gopher menus and allows the user to search the menus for words. Programs such as these have found widespread use in academic and industrial settings.

The newest and for most users the best method for using the Internet is the World Wide Web. First developed at the European Particle Physics Laboratory in Geneva, Switzerland, the Web is now maintained and enhanced at the National Center for Supercomputing Applications at the University of Illinois. The Web consists of a large and rapidly growing number of *sites* on the Internet that are easy to get to, easy to use, and pleasing to the eye.

Special utility programs are available to help you negotiate the Web. *Browsers* such as Netscape Navigator and Internet Explorer give you quick access to the multiple sites on the Web. In turn, Web sites such as Yahoo (http://www.yahoo.com), which was one of the first of its kind, have powerful programs called "search engines" that let you explore the vast resources of the Internet by typing words representing topics of interest. And the Web has do-it-yourself capabilities; with relative ease, you can create your own site on the Internet, with text and color graphics if you wish, for others to browse. Web technology has greatly augmented the use of the Internet. It has been predicted that by the year 2000, over a hundred million people will have access to computer-based telecommunication. As a cautionary note, I might point out that browsing the Internet can be addictive. There is even a self-help group for excessive users (Web site unknown).

Other On-Line Services

During the 1980s, computer-based information services in addition to the Internet appeared on-line for use by anyone with a personal computer, modem, telephone line, funds to pay for the service (typically a modest monthly rate), funds to pay for so-called extended services, which are sometimes the most desirable and can be quite expensive (in the range of $15 per hour), and a willingness to tolerate the many advertisements that accompany the programs. CompuServe, the first; Prodigy, which came later; and America Online, the newest, are the three most prominent of these services, and each offers a large array of its own programs as well as a route to the resources of the Internet.

MEDICINE ON-LINE

By whatever means of access, more and more medical information is available by computer-based telecommunication—more and more medicine is on-line. For the patient, Web sites offer a wide range of health-related information. Yahoo, for example, offers access to more than two thousand health sites. When you as the user select *Health: Medicine, Drugs, Diseases, Fitness* you are presented with an initial menu of thirty-seven categories (growing all the time), in alphabetical order, beginning with Alternative Medicine, Career and Employment, Companies, and Death and Dying, and ending with Travel, Weight Issues, Women's Health, and Workplace. Each of these categories, in turn, will direct you to numerous subcategories as you home in on the health site of your particular interest. If you select Women's Health, you get a menu of thirteen categories, beginning with AIDS/HIV and ending with Reproductive Health. If you then choose AIDS/HIV, you are directed to a long list of AIDS-related newsletters, compiled from a variety of sources, ranging from the Food and Drug Administration to various pharmaceutical companies.

For the most part, such information is unidirectional, presented in a noninteractive and didactic manner; much of what is available on the Web sites for patients is also available in pamphlets and other printed documents. And as with all health-related literature directed to the patient, the reader must be wary of the source and seek second and third opinions. Misinformation and unfounded opinion are there along with the useful and well founded; there is very little censorship on the Internet. But the information is there in abundance and its accessibility is unparalleled in the history of civilization.

Virtually anyone can have access to a vast amount of potentially useful information, or at least anyone with access to a library that offers the Internet or with sufficient means to own the appropriate hardware and software. And the costs keep coming down. Once only the government and large corporate institutions could afford a computer. Now most middle-income families can afford a personal computer with modem. As I write, you can go on-line, with no frills, for about $1,000 and some personal guidance from someone who is already there. There is even a modification that will bring the Internet to your television set, and as with the rest of the technology, its price is dropping. Soon you will be able to sign on at home for no more than a few hundred dollars. I can only hope that computer-based telecommunication will continue to evolve in the manner of the handheld calculator, which just about anyone can own these days. The computer may have started out in the hands of the elite, but it is now available to more and more people of all backgrounds; it is becoming democratized as well as democratizing.

But let us turn now to what is perhaps the most powerful *and* empowering function of computer-based telecommunication—conversation by computer.

Teleconverse

Much of telecommunication is one way, with messages sent for which no reply is expected. There is a form, however, that is deserving of its own name, and I call it "teleconverse." This is long-distance *conversation*—the exchange of messages between people by way of the computer. Electronic mail is the earliest—and still most prevalent—form of teleconverse.

In the early days of ARPANET, computer-based network technology was used primarily for sending large files of information back and forth at relatively slow rates of transmission. As things speeded up, however, messages and replies to messages were sometimes included with these packets of information. With time, short messages began to supersede large documents. Driven by its users in this way, ARPANET spawned an embryonic form of teleconverse, which in a gestational period of a few years developed into electronic mail.

Someone once noted that the best place to pave a path is where the grass is worn and people are already walking, not where you think people *ought* to walk. With computer-based telecommunication, the path being used was electronic mail. No one was telling people they *had* to use electronic mail; they were using it because the technology was available and it was a helpful form of day-to-day conversation. And now, with the Internet much faster than it used to be, teleconverse by electronic mail has become the most heavily used of the Internet capabilities. Furthermore, virtually all the on-line services, such as CompuServe, Prodigy, and America Online, offer their own versions of electronic mail, as well as access to the Internet, and multiple electronic mail programs are available for smaller networks of computers.

Electronic mail on the Internet serves many people in many different ways. Let me address a few of them by way of example.

INDIVIDUAL MAILINGS AND POSTINGS. Any person with access to the Internet, by any means, can use electronic mail. You must be able to type, but not by any formal method. You can send me a message right now if you like, at wslack@bih.harvard.edu, and I will do my best to respond. You could also send a message to Tom Ferguson, at DrTomHI@aol.com, who specializes in self-care programs and wrote *Health Online*, which is an excellent guide to on-line services for patients and prospective patients and the most useful resource to date in the field, in my opinion. Or you could send a message to both Tom and me at the same time, or to a larger group still.

Then there are the news groups, which serve as electronic bulletin boards. Unlike users of personal e-mail, who receive their messages unsolicited, participants in news groups must request access to the postings of their group, just as they would go to a bulletin board to read messages. After reading a posted message, a user can add a comment to what has been said, introduce a new topic, or initiate a call for help. There are thousands of news groups, with material on a staggering number of topics, many of them health-related. Self-help groups are well represented. People with a wide variety of physical, emotional, and social problems use their news groups to give and receive advice and support, even in times of emergency. People contemplating suicide have turned to a news group for help. Some of the groups are moderated by a person who reads and edits the incoming messages before posting them for general reading. But most of them have no moderator, so that all postings are available for all to read and respond to. Messages can be personalized, however; a user can send an e-mail message directly to the originator of a posted news group message to be read only by him or her.

This is a powerful means of communication. I use it often to communicate with colleagues, friends, and family. It is difficult to estimate the number of medically related messages that flow between people, day in and day out, but it must be very large.

THE SELF-HELP MAILING LIST. The mailing list, as it is called in Internet parlance, is somewhat different. First there is the list owner, or facilitator, who has an interest in a particular topic, a medical topic for our purposes. The facilitator announces that he or she is founding a mailing list on this topic, and electronic mail users who share this person's interest submit their electronic mail addresses as a means of becoming members. Members can send messages to the list for distribution; the facilitator either forwards the messages directly to the other members, or compiles them into an electronic mail newsletter, which is then sent to members at regular intervals. With many mailing lists, an automatic "mail server" compiles the messages and sends them out unedited. This saves the facilitator's time and eliminates the possibility of censorship. On the other hand, the product is often more cumbersome and less substantive than a cogent newsletter prepared by a careful editor.

Hundreds of self-help support group mailing lists are already available to those who have the equipment and inclination to search for one and sign up, and the number is growing all the time. If you are interested in a topic, in this case, health-related, and would like to discuss it with other people, medical or nonmedical, you can probably find an appropriate group. Were they alive, Bill W. and Dr. Bob might be very pleased to discover that Alcoholics Anonymous is well represented, as is Al-Anon. From AIDS and Alzheimer's disease to stroke, stuttering, and yeast infections, a large array of medical conditions are represented by on-line groups. Formed, maintained, and driven by users, this is patient power of the first order.

The way a mailing list works when used well—people communicating as peers with the common goal of helping each other—is perhaps best exemplified by a quote from Samantha Scolamiero, founder of BRAINTMR, the brain tumor mailing list. This quote evolved from a series of e-mail messages and personal conversations between Samantha and Tom Ferguson, which I reprint (with a few revisions) from *Health Online* with their permission:

> As a brain tumor survivor, I began BRAINTMR in 1993 with the simple hope of helping people concerned with brain tumors to share information and experiences. In a short time BRAINTMR has moved far beyond that initial vision.
>
> Of our 1,000 members, roughly three fourths are patients and family members. We share information and advice about the best medical centers, about little-known clinical trials, nutrition, rehabilitation, alternative therapies, doctor/patient relationships, and other resources on the Internet. Patients use printouts of list messages to get their doctors to help them join the latest clinical trials.
>
> As one subscriber explained, "The issues and problems we deal with on the list are more specific and realistic than information gathered from books, articles, and other sources." By sharing wisdom gained during their brain tumor ordeal, patients and families help one another to cope and to feel empowered. The list helps to ease isolation and depression and provides a coping strategy for difficult times. People who might be intimidated by face-to-face meetings can participate in a friendly, mutually supportive exchange. BRAINTMR is a welcome

haven for those with no local group. And with adaptive input/output equipment, even those who are disabled can participate.

About one fourth of our members are neurosurgeons, nurses, psychologists, epidemiologists, pathologists, social workers, and other clinicians and researchers. Our doctor members have told me that monitoring the list helps *them* understand the specific physical, emotional, and spiritual needs of their patients [italics mine]. Such insights can be difficult in the midst of a busy clinical practice.

Countless printouts from our list circulate among brain tumor specialists. One list participant, a faculty member at a major U.S. brain tumor research center, routinely forwards list messages to forty-eight colleagues. Armed with our printouts, an oncologist in a developing country convinces colleagues to try new treatment options.

List members—laypeople and professionals alike—have moved beyond the old, obsolete mindset that holds that only certain "qualified" medical professionals may create and disseminate medical information. We are showing that we are qualified through our experience. We now see that we are capable of contributions no professional can make, and that by linking our efforts in a coordinated team, we can advance the well-being of all.

By breaking down the rigid social boundaries that traditionally exist between doctors, patients, and researchers, the BRAINTMR mailing list is pointing the way toward a new type of participatory medicine in which *all* those concerned with a given health problem can work together as colleagues to promote healing and well-being.

Samantha J. Scolamiero
Founder and facilitator
BRAINTMR mailing list
samajane@sasquatch.com

In addition, Rand Hove, a user of BRAINTMR, wrote a series of electronic mail messages to Samantha, which are summarized here with his permission:

BRAINTMR is the best service I have seen, which makes the technological commodity of electronic information intensely vital, powerful, and human. . . . BRAINTMR is illuminating some very dark and frightening places for people who are in urgent need. . . . Here, electronic communication has its greatest value, making us more real and tangible, as opposed to having the dehumanizing effect computers are notorious for. . . . We are the people who are changing the definition of community for the 21st century.

Rand Hove, Brain Tumor Survivor, Minnesota

SELF-HELP CHAT GROUPS. Chat groups offer people the opportunity to converse with each other electronically at the same time. Whereas electronic mail messages to individuals and lists of people can be sent at any time of day or night, which is an important convenience when senders and receivers have different schedules, chat groups require coordinated schedules. On the other hand, they provide a valuable means of real-time communication. For example, the Web site for the Juvenile Diabetes Foundation now offers chat-group access to the parents of a diabetic child, who tell me this has already become a very helpful resource.

AIDS On-Line

AIDS is well represented on the Internet. The Web site of the Centers for Disease Control and Prevention (http://www.cdcnac.org) offers current information about prevention and treatment, news about AIDS-related services, and directions to nineteen additional AIDS-related Web sites. New Riders' *Internet Yellow Pages* has eight listings, each of which leads to multiple sources of further information. And most important, there are numerous news groups, mailing lists, and chat groups that help patients and doctors keep themselves and each other informed. Like other self-help support groups on the Internet, AIDS groups have been an important source of patient power. They have enabled people from widely dispersed geographic areas to make a coordinated effort to put pressure on agencies that could help with both treatment and AIDS-related research.

Good News and Bad

As with all forms of communication, there are bad messages on electronic mail as well as good ones. There is a natural tendency to single out the problems people have with new technology as if they were unique, when upon reflection it is clear that they were there with the old technology as well. People worry about rudeness on the Internet, and it is there. But so is there rudeness on the telephone. Good manners do not always prevail with electronic mail, but this is not the fault of the medium; it is the fault of the message. We should insist on courtesy as we interact with others on electronic mail.

Not all mailing lists work out as a member might hope. There may be too many messages to read; there may be useless, angry (*flaming*, in Internet parlance), or insulting messages. On the other hand, it is as easy to unsubscribe as it is to subscribe. Membership is voluntary. And if you don't like what you see, you can always start your own mailing list. Electronic mail on the Internet is the First Amendment in action; it is participatory democracy at its best.

There is no governmental regulatory agency for mailing lists as yet, and I hope there never will be. In the spirit of self-help, let the Internet remain self-regulatory.

———~~~———

Early prophets of doom—"patients will refuse to have anything to do with a computer"—have been proved wrong. The burgeoning use of the Internet for medical matters attests to the fact that patients *like* to be on-line. And if they don't, they don't have to be. But what about the clinician? Will the clinician go on-line?

PART TWO

The Computer
and the Clinician

CHAPTER SIX

Computing
for the Hospital

~~~

In spite of a tendency to be conservative in many ways, twentieth-century physicians have tended to be liberal in their use of new technology. Unfortunately, as we have learned along the way, technological innovations in medicine sometimes do more harm than good. As I have noted earlier, X rays were used to treat enlarged thymus glands, ringworm, and acne before the dangers of irradiation were well known. I can remember the fluoroscope machines that were put in shoe stores so that customers could watch the bones of their feet moving inside their shoes. It is important for us to proceed with caution as we use any new technique, including the computer, in the care of patients.

On the other hand, sometimes the most notable side effect of a technological innovation is the break with tradition that its use entails. This is not likely to be of concern to the individual patient, who is interested primarily in getting well, or the individual doctor, who is interested primarily in helping patients get well, but from a collective standpoint there can be something disturbing about altering the status quo. After René Laënnec invented the stethoscope in 1816, physicians stopped placing an ear against the patient's chest, ending a long tradition. The change was criticized in the London *Times*: "That [the stethoscope] will ever come into general use notwithstanding its value is extremely doubtful, because its beneficial application requires much time and gives a good bit of trouble to the patient and to the practitioner, and because its hue and character are foreign and opposed to our habits and associations. There is something even ludicrous in the picture of a grave physician proudly listening through a long tube applied to the patient's thorax."

Just as the now-anonymous voice in the London *Times* worried about the use of the stethoscope in medicine in the nineteenth century, there are those who worry about the use of the computer in medicine. In the early 1960s, with the increased availability of digital computers, many doctors were concerned about the potential encroachment of this new technology on the profession of medicine and on the traditional rapport between doctor and patient. There were well-meaning Luddites among us, ready to suppress any electronic addition to the practice of medicine. The debate was frequently lively, and a commonly asked question was "Will your computer replace the doctor?" A rejoinder that I found useful, one borrowed from psychologists working with teaching machines, was that any doctor who could be replaced by a computer deserved to be.

IS THE COMPUTER IMMORAL?

There are still some among us today who worry about the computer in medicine, particularly if to use the computer is to alter the doctor-patient relationship. To them the doctor-patient relationship has intrinsic value, independent of diagnosis and treatment, and any program that interferes with this relationship should be avoided, regardless of its potential benefit to the patient.

Consider for a moment the program Eliza, which interacted with the user in a manner suggestive of nondirective therapy. Developed by Joseph Weizenbaum of MIT in the 1960s, the program was impressive for its time, and those who tried it found it interesting and entertaining. Later, however, Weizenbaum stepped back from his console and attributed dangerousness to his program. After that, he argued against the use of interactive programs in medicine, including some of mine.

Focusing on a system (similar to his own) developed by Kenneth Colby and colleagues, Weizenbaum expressed particular concern about the use of computers for psychotherapy, which he considered not only dangerous but immoral—indeed, "simply obscene." He wrote, "These are [programs] whose very contemplation ought to give rise to feelings of disgust in every civilized person. . . . I would put all projects that propose to substitute a computer system for a human function that involves interpersonal respect, understanding, and love in this category. I therefore reject Colby's proposal that computers be installed as psychotherapists, *not on the grounds that such a project might be technically infeasible* [italics mine], but on the grounds that it is immoral."

Most of the patients I have known, "civilized" or not, would value relief from illness more highly than a relationship with a therapist. Yet Weizenbaum appears to think that the possibility of obtaining respect, understanding, and love in the clinic is more important. Does he really mean to say that if an interactive computer could help a patient with anxiety or depression (or cancer or AIDS), that would be obscene?

If therapy based on an interpersonal relationship is the best we have to offer, and certainly there are medical problems for which this is the case, then respect and understanding (perhaps sometimes even love) are essential to the relationship. Of course, respect and understanding are important in *all* interactions between doctor and patient, even when procedures such as patient-computer dialogue are used in conjunction with the clinician's care. But if an approach to therapy, with or without the computer, can be shown to be more effective, less costly, or more convenient than therapy based on a doctor-patient relationship, I think most patients would take their chances on finding respect, understanding, and love outside the clinic.

The problem is not, as Weizenbaum and those who share his philosophy erroneously conclude, that computers in medicine are dangerous or immoral; the problem is that they have yet to reach their full potential. Instead of attacking the *idea* of using patient-computer dialogue in clinical care, which even Weizenbaum knew might be technically feasible, let those of us in the field concentrate our efforts on developing programs that work well on behalf of the patient.

A HISTORICAL PERSPECTIVE ON CLINICAL COMPUTING

Coupled with early concerns about the computer in medicine was excessive admiration. There is a sociological principle, often true, that people tend to react to new technology with unreasonable expectations as well as fear. The electronic digital computer, with its capacity to hold and process large amounts of information with great speed and accuracy, was indeed an awe-inspiring device—one that stimulated comparisons with the brain itself and fostered remarkable prophecies.

For most people, fear of the computer in medicine waned as the great expectations increased and prophecy became a substitute for accomplishment. Computer manufacturers, in turn, moved to capitalize on these great expectations. Some advertised their machines as panaceas for the medical community; they sold what they called total hospital information systems that were at best partial and contained remarkably little information. When the dust settled, in part on expensive, unused computer terminals, hospitals that had purchased these systems found that they had spent a great deal of money and received little in return—usually partially working billing systems. From the patient's perspective, the principal difference was that the bills, although higher because of the computing costs, arrived, if at all, somewhat later than before.

Typically, financial data were recorded throughout the hospital on pieces of paper, aggregated in a data processing area, keypunched onto Hollerith cards or magnetic media, and fed to the computer. From these data, the computer produced bills for patients or third-party payers, payment checks for the hospital's creditors and employees, and a very large number of printed reports. Computers programmed to handle batches of financial transactions have proved poorly suited to interactive clinical applications, and have had little impact on the practice of medicine.

Pioneers in Clinical Computing

In the 1960s, however, a small but growing number of people from the United States, Canada, Great Britain, Europe, and Asia, primarily clinicians and computer scientists in medical schools and teaching hospitals, began to work actively with computers in medicine. Virtually all clinical computing in those days was restricted to large clinical institutions. There were no desktop, let alone laptop, machines.

Supported for the most part by government grants, these pioneers got their own machines and used principles from a wide variety of disciplines, including arithmetic, symbolic logic, Boolean logic, algebra, probability, linguistics, statistics, and the theory of games. They studied the computer as a diagnostician; as an interpreter of images, such as electrocardiograms, electroencephalograms, and X-ray films; and as a teaching machine for students and clinicians in training. And they demonstrated that the needs of individual clinical departments such as the admitting office, the medical records department, the pharmacy, the pathology department, and the radiology department could successfully be served by computers. With few exceptions, these programs were electronically isolated from one another, or interfaced in such a manner that they could not readily share information, yet they pioneered the introduction of computing into the hospital environment.

Also in the 1960s, stand-alone computers began to appear in the laboratories of hospitals and clinics. They were used to collect test results from the automatic analyzers, print the results on paper forms for distribution to the clinicians for use in patient care, assist in maintaining the accuracy of the diagnostic machines that produced the results (a process called quality control), and capture charges for use in billing patients or their third-party payers. Today, many hospitals and clinics have such computing systems in one or more of their laboratories and clinical departments.

The Chip in the Laboratory

The evolution of the automatic analyzers in the clinical laboratories and the machines used in the clinical departments such as cardiology, neurology, and radiology is a story of rapidly advancing computer technology of a different nature. Embedded in these machines are the chip and microchip, the building blocks of all computers, containing large amounts of electronic circuitry. The machines used for diagnostic procedures, such as electrocardiography (ECG) and cardiac catheterization in the cardiology department, electroencephalography (EEG) and electromyography (EMG) in neurology, and X rays, ultrasound, magnetic resonance imaging (MRI), and, by definition, computerized axial tomography (CAT scanning) in radiology all have built-in computers. The CAT scan and MRI, which provide exquisitely detailed images of soft tissues, organs, and organ systems, are high on my list of important medical inventions of the twentieth century. These noninvasive methods have replaced draconian procedures such as the pneumoencephalogram, which involved withdrawing spinal fluid with a needle and replacing it with air. The air would float into the cavities of the brain, permitting the structures to be seen on X-ray. Having done this painful and lengthy procedure on children as well as adults, I particularly appreciate the new machines.

We don't tend to think of these machines as part of clinical computing, or cybermedicine as I am calling this rapidly growing discipline, and they are not the subject of this book. But it is helpful to keep in mind that the most pervasive use of computing technology in medicine to date is the microchip in the diagnostic machine.

Reporting Results

On the other hand, the results of diagnostic studies generated in the laboratories and clinical departments are still, for the most part, not readily available to the clinicians who need them. The results are typically printed on paper as they are generated and then distributed for use at a later time. In most settings, the doctor must await the distribution of the printed reports, which are known to arrive late and sometimes not at all.

Unfortunately, the use of the computer in direct dialogue with the doctor to communicate the results of diagnostic studies is still more the exception than the rule. Doctor-computer dialogue has a lot of catching up to do. But I get ahead of myself.

COMPUTING SYSTEMS IN
TWO TEACHING HOSPITALS

Computers in medicine were still used mostly for financial purposes when, in 1970, I moved from the University of Wisconsin in Madison to join Howard Bleich in the Department of Medicine of the Harvard Medical School in Boston. Howard and I had different clinical interests (he was trained in nephrology, I in neurology), but we shared a common enthusiasm for the use of the computer in medicine.

A New Division

With the invaluable support of Howard Hiatt, who was head of Harvard's Department of Medicine at Beth Israel Hospital, Howard Bleich and I established a division of clinical computing in the department, analogous to divisions such as cardiology, endocrinology, and gastroenterology. We devoted our efforts during the 1970s to research in clinical computing, supported by grants from the federal government. Howard studied the use of the computer to interact directly with the doctor to collect, store, and analyze information of diagnostic importance and to offer the doctor advice and suggestions about diagnosis and treatment. I continued my studies of patient-computer dialogue.

In 1976, Howard and I approached the administration of the hospital with a plan to develop, not isolated computer applications for individual departments, but a single, hospital-wide clinical computing system. Our primary purpose was to use the computer to help doctors, nurses, and other clinicians provide better care for patients. We were convinced, however, that the finances of the hospital would also benefit from the system. At the time, we were most fortunate to have Robert Beckley join our division. Bob would provide technical leadership for the project, both at Beth Israel and Brigham and Women's hospitals.

Seven Principles

We had seven principles in mind at the outset—criteria for a successful system that of course are clearer in our minds now, post hoc, than they were when we were getting started.

• *Information should be captured directly at computer terminals located at the point of each transaction, not on pieces of paper.* If the information is generated by an automated device, such as a laboratory analyzer, the machine should be connected electronically to the computer, which in turn should help determine the reliability and accuracy of the results. If the information must be entered manually, the computer should provide immediate benefit to the person who must enter this information.

• *Information captured at a terminal or automated device anywhere in the hospital or clinic should be available immediately, if needed, at any other terminal.* Rather than printed reports, which become progressively out of date from the moment they are produced, terminals that provide immediate access to the most up-to-date information should be the principal means of retrieval.

• *The response time of the computer should be rapid.* For the busy physician, nurse, or medical technologist, delays that can be measured in seconds are often unacceptable.

• *The computer should be reliable and accurate.* In the event of failure, the defect should be corrected within minutes, and users should never lose data.

- *Confidentiality should be protected.* Only authorized persons should have access to the data.
- *The computer programs should be friendly to the user and reinforce the user's behavior.* There should be no need for users' manuals. The programs should be self-explanatory. Howard and I have a theorem that the quality of any computer program is *inversely* proportionate to the size of the manual sitting next to the terminal.
- *There should be a common registry for all patients.* For each patient there should be one and only one set of identifying information in the computer, available at all times to authorized users and preserved, if possible, in perpetuity. Whenever an error in the common database is detected and corrected at any terminal, that correction should be immediately available at all terminals. The common registry should be shared throughout the hospital by all programs that involve identification of a patient.

In collaboration with our colleagues in the hospital, we developed and installed a hospital-wide clinical computing system that we believe fulfilled these criteria, at least for the most part. In the fall of 1982, on the basis of experience gained at Beth Israel Hospital, we were asked to develop a similar computing system at Boston's Brigham and Women's Hospital. Shortly thereafter, we formed the Center for Clinical Computing (CCC), which was staffed by the highly talented group of programmers and engineers who had worked with us to develop the system at Beth Israel, as well as new people who joined us to work on the system at Brigham and Women's. The development of the computing systems for the two hospitals was then under the direction of the CCC.

In the paragraphs that follow, I will describe these systems, which to this day are heavily used and well received by those who use them. These are certainly not the only hospital-wide clinical computing systems. Excellent programs, such as those at the Kaiser Permanente hospitals in California, LDS Hospital in Salt Lake City, the Regenstrief Institute in Indianapolis, Geneva University, Leiden University Hospital in the Netherlands, and the Columbia-Presbyterian Hospital in New York, have proved to be highly useful in the practice of medicine.

The Two Hospitals

Beth Israel and Brigham and Women's hospitals are both teaching hospitals of the Harvard Medical School. Beth Israel has 480 beds,

60 bassinets, and an active emergency room. Each year there are approximately thirty thousand admissions and two hundred thousand outpatient visits. Brigham and Women's Hospital has 739 beds, 96 bassinets, and an active emergency room. Each year there are approximately thirty-five thousand admissions and five hundred thousand outpatient visits. Both hospitals have active teaching programs with medical students, interns, residents, and clinical fellows on every medical and surgical service; and both hospitals have active research programs in each of their academic departments.

The programs that provide clinical computing were written initially in the MIIS dialect (from Medical Information Technology, Inc.) of MUMPS and have run on separate networks of Data General minicomputers, one network at each hospital. There are over four thousand computer terminals at each of the two hospitals and its related clinics.

Admitting, Outpatient, and Medical Records Departments

At both hospitals, the first components of the clinical computing systems were implemented in the admitting, outpatient, and medical records departments. These registration programs make up the core of the systems. Although the computer programs were tailored to the individual needs of each hospital, the programs were similar in function. For each of over 1 million patients cared for at Beth Israel Hospital since its system of medical record numbers was established in 1966, and for each of over 1.5 million patients at Brigham and Women's Hospital, the name, address, telephone number, social security number, and the names of the parents and spouse are stored in the computers in common registries, a separate one for each hospital.

For the purpose of understanding how the computing works, picture yourself, if you will, as a person newly arrived in Boston. You have a new doctor who is on the staff of one of the two hospitals and has referred you there for an appointment. When you arrive as a new patient, whether as an inpatient or an outpatient, a receptionist interviews you and enters your identifying information, in your presence, at a computer terminal. Registration can occur at any of multiple stations throughout the hospitals.

Once your name and other identifying information are in the registry, they stay there indefinitely; thereafter, initiation of a hospital admission, outpatient visit, or major clinical procedure requires only that someone check and update your information. This is convenient for the receptionist and saves your time as well. It is also more friendly.

If you change your name, address, or other identifying information, corrections can be made, in your presence with your approval, at any terminal by any authorized person who has access to the registry; however, the system preserves an audit trail of the information entered previously, which can be displayed if a question of accuracy arises.

In the admitting departments, staff use terminals for your preadmission (if you are scheduled for hospitalization), to note the time of your arrival, and to keep track of your transfer to different rooms and clinical services, when the occasions arise. Unusual circumstances must be accommodated. If you are admitted inadvertently, there is an Unadmit option; if you are discharged inadvertently, there is an Undischarge option. Because your current location is known to the computer, meals, mail, medications, laboratory reports, and visitors are all guided correctly to your room.

In the outpatient departments, staff use terminals to note your arrival and to schedule future visits. The computer applies special rules defined for each clinic to make your appointment; by keeping track of all appointments, it keeps conflicts for both you and your doctor to a minimum. In the operating rooms, staff use terminals to schedule surgical procedures for inpatients and outpatients, and to follow your location in the preoperative, operating, and recovery rooms.

Medical Records

In the medical records departments, light pens, which read barcoded labels, keep track of your paper chart as it is signed out and returned to the department. (The paper chart, though still in existence, is destined for extinction as records become more fully electronic.) Your chart can be requested from any terminal in either hospital by an authorized person participating in your care. Each request generates a ticket, printed in the medical records department, which provides the last-known location of your chart. Personnel no longer go to shelves jammed with charts only to learn that yours is somewhere else. If you are scheduled to be admitted or seen the next day, the system automatically prints out a request for your chart the night before. If you were to show up in one of the emergency rooms unexpectedly, a request for immediate delivery of your chart would pop out of the printer in the medical records department automatically as soon as the computer received notice of your arrival.

DIAGNOSTIC STUDIES

Once the registration programs were up and running, programs in virtually every laboratory and clinical department were developed and integrated with the registration programs. Gary Horowitz would provide the leadership for these programs. Consider yourself, if you will, still to be a patient in the hospital.

Laboratories

Computer terminals in the hematology, chemistry, virology, endocrinology, immunology, and microbiology laboratories communicate with the common registry of patients, and your name can be readily located within the registry when you are having laboratory tests performed. When your specimen arrives, such as blood or urine, the technologist identifies you in the registry and indicates which tests have been requested by your doctor. The computer in turn assigns an accession number, notes the date and time, and prints labels and work sheets as required.

In Thomas O'Brien's microbiology laboratory at Brigham and Women's Hospital, where your urine might be cultured for a bacterial infection, there are no printed work sheets. Instead, the computer program, designed by Sandra Goodman and her coworkers, interacts directly with the technologist, presenting each protocol to be followed in a manner individualized for the suspected organisms. If bacteria are cultured from your urine, their descriptions, together with their sensitivities to antimicrobial agents that could be used for your treatment, are entered directly at the terminals at the time the results are determined; these data are then available to your doctor upon request from any terminal in the hospital or in his or her office.

Automated devices in the laboratories connect to the computer networks electronically. Results of studies obtained with these devices, such as your blood count and blood sugar, are first displayed on terminals in the laboratories, where a technologist checks them. If you have had a blood count in the recent past, the results of that count appear next to the current ones; on occasion, a marked disparity between a recent and current result has enabled the technologist to detect a mislabeled specimen or the effect of an interfering substance causing an error in the test. If the results of your test are markedly abnormal or the current result is substantially different from the previous determination, the computer automatically flags the results; such results would then be rechecked by a senior technologist and telephoned to your doctor at the number provided by the computer. In this way, the computer helps to ensure the quality of tests performed. Once verified, the results of your tests are released for viewing by your doctor at any of the terminals located throughout the hospitals and outpatient clinics.

Clinical Departments

Cardiology, neurology, pathology, and radiology are representative of departments that have been computerized. In the exercise, echocardiography, and cardiac catheterization laboratories, the technologist would use the computer to identify you in the registry and to indicate the procedure to be performed. The results of your study, a cardiac catheterization, for example, if you are a middle-aged man with heart trouble, would then be recorded at a terminal and approved by a staff cardiologist. Before the computer system was in place, weeks or sometimes months might pass before your results would find their way to your chart; results are now available within a few days, both for viewing on terminals and for placement in your paper chart.

If an electrocardiogram is indicated at Beth Israel Hospital, your doctor uses a terminal at a nursing station or in his or her office to request the study. Your identifying information is then electronically transferred to the electrocardiography chart for use at the time of your study. Once the results have been approved, they are transferred electronically to the hospital's computers, which make the verbal report (with the electrocardiogram itself if your doctor is using a PC) available for viewing.

In the neurology department at Beth Israel Hospital, technologists in the electroencephalography, electromyography, and evoked potential laboratories can use the computer to identify you in the registry, to indicate the study to be performed, and to record the results of your study, which are then approved by a staff neurologist and made available for viewing on the hospital's terminals.

In the surgical pathology departments, where biopsy specimens are examined, and the cytology department, where Pap tests are performed, every specimen is registered in the computer; if you have had specimens analyzed previously, the program provides the identification numbers so that the slides can be retrieved and reexamined under the microscope. Anatomical and microscopical descriptions of each new specimen are transcribed into a word processor in the computer. The pathologist then reviews and edits this report at any available terminal, and as with all the diagnostic studies, releases the report for viewing on terminals throughout the hospital.

And so it is in radiology. When you are about to have a chest X-ray at Beth Israel Hospital, the receptionist identifies you at a terminal and denotes the examination. The computer then prints a work card for the technologist, a label for the new film jacket, a transportation ticket that provides your room number (if you are hospitalized), and an identification card that is optically photographed to label the new films at the time of the X-ray exposure. At the same time, a printer located in the file room produces a request to retrieve your previous films.

When the technologist indicates at a terminal that your examination has been completed, the computer automatically adds the charge for your films to your hospital bill—a function more in the hospital's interest than yours. As your films (the front and side views) emerge from the dryer, they are merged with any previous films you may have had and presented to your radiologist for interpretation and side-by-side comparison. The radiologist will then record his or her diagnostic interpretation directly at a terminal with an interactive coding system developed in the radiology department by Morris Simon, Brian Leeming, Jerry Jackson, and their coworkers. (Some radiologists prefer to dictate their reports, which are then transcribed into a word processor on the same computer.) Your radiologist would then use the terminal to edit and approve the report, which would then be released for viewing by authorized clinicians in patient care areas throughout the hospital and clinics.

Programs in virtually every laboratory and department devoted to treatment have also been developed and integrated with the registration systems. The blood banks and the pharmacies are two examples.

BLOOD BANK. In the blood banks, where donated blood is stored and distributed for use in transfusions, the programs maintain data in case you should need a blood transfusion. The data include your transfusion history—Have you ever had one? Have you ever had a problem with a transfusion?—your blood type and associated antibodies, and any specific requirements you might have, such as the need for blood that has been irradiated or is low in white blood cells. If you are about to have surgery, this information is automatically transmitted to the blood bank from the program that scheduled your operating room.

The terminals are also used to maintain an inventory of blood that is available for use. When your doctor requests blood for you, the computer helps find the most appropriate units, looking first for autologous blood (if you have previously donated your own blood), then for blood that has been cross-matched and held in reserve for you, and finally for blood that is most likely to be suitable for you on the basis of your type, the antibodies in your blood, and any specific requirements you might have.

PHARMACY. Under the direction of Richard Pope in the early days of the CCC system, the pharmacy computing system serves an important role. At each hospital, the computers maintain the *formularies*—the lists of available medications. If your doctor requests medications for you while you are in the hospital, the computer helps to organize the preparation and distribution of your medications, whether they are to be taken by mouth or intravenously. A list of each of your medications is then made available for viewing on terminals throughout the hospital. The computers also assist with inventory by permitting surveillance of available medications, both according to manufacturer and according to functional class.

Financial Computing

Virtually every one of the services provided to you, whether it is your outpatient visit, inpatient admission, diagnostic study, medication order, or blood transfusion, must be registered in the computer before it can be performed. Manual registration and identification procedures that were once used throughout the hospitals—procedures that were fraught with error and lost charges—have largely disappeared. After the service has been performed and its results have been recorded in the computer, the charge is automatically added to your file. In this way, more than 90 percent of the charges are obtained as a by-product of the clinical computing systems.

At Beth Israel Hospital, these charges are transferred by magnetic tape each day to the hospital's fiscal computing system (in a separate facility not in the CCC network), which prints the bills and performs other financial operations.

At Brigham and Women's Hospital, the billing office is integrated with the clinical computing network. The clinical computing system produces billing tapes, both for inpatients and outpatients, that are transferred to third-party payers, such as Medicare, Medicaid, and Blue Cross. In turn, remittance tapes from third-party payers, which accompany the payment checks, are read by the computer and used to match the payment received with your account.

Other financial programs on Brigham and Women's network include a general ledger program that accumulates financial data needed for managers; a purchasing program that maintains an inventory of supplies, keeps track of vendors, and computes the amount owed to the hospital's suppliers; and a personnel program that stores data regarding employees and computes their paychecks.

At each hospital, the computer assigns a diagnosis-related group (DRG) to each patient and alerts the medical records department when additional coding may entitle the hospital to increased reimbursement. At Beth Israel Hospital, the computer prints reminders listing the abnormal laboratory results of patients on Medicare that may entitle the hospital to additional reimbursement.

It is important to keep in mind, however, that when third parties, such as the government, managed care agencies, and insurance companies pay the medical bills, they ask for clinical information to justify the payments. This creates a breach in the confidential relationship between you and your doctor. But this is the topic of a later chapter.

New Horizons

In 1989, upon completion of the CCC project at Brigham and Women's Hospital, administrative responsibility for computing was transferred to the hospital. Since that time, clinicians and programmers there have developed a number of new clinical computing programs. In 1995, administrative control was also transferred to Beth Israel Hospital, where computing systems are now being converted to new machines and computer programming languages. The new technology should provide more modern visual presentation to the user, together with increased speed and efficiency.

On the other hand, my colleagues at the two hospitals and in the CCC prefer to have clinical computing systems judged on the basis of how well they work, how useful they are, and how frugally they run. In these days of computing glitz, where the computer culturati flaunt their jargon with an Orwellian facileness (try *client server, open systems, data warehouse,* and *connectivity* for starters), where new computing and new words to describe it (for example, *best of breed*) are considered desirable solely because they are new, even when the computing is outperformed by the old (*legacy system* in the newest computerspeak), it is helpful to ask the old question, "What is the problem we are trying to solve?"

The problem we are trying to solve with the computer in medicine is a problem in communication—the current insufficiency of readily available information that could help clinicians care for patients. If the computer can be programmed to communicate with the doctor, at his or her beck and call, to provide the results of diagnostic studies, offer advice and consultation, and give access to articles in medical journals, the doctor and patient will be well served, even if the technology behind the computer terminal is behind the times. The patient in pain is less interested in three-dimensional color graphics than in competent care.

—⁘—

The ultimate goal of hospital computing is to improve patient care. Sometimes this gets forgotten. Sometimes the computing in an individual department becomes an end in itself, independent of the collective goal of patient care. The goal in the clinical laboratory is not to have a well-run laboratory in isolation from the rest of the hospital; the goal is to get the results of diagnostic studies to the doctor, with accuracy and reliability. The goal in finance is not to make money; the goal is to support good medical care.

In most hospitals and clinics to this day, the computing is mostly financial, under the auspices of the chief financial officer, and managerial, under the auspices of a chief information officer. The acronym MIS stands for *Management* Information Systems, not *Medical.* It is my abiding hope that the "M" in MIS will soon stand for "Medical."

When the "M" does stand for "Medical," what will this mean for the doctor?

CHAPTER SEVEN

Computing for the Clinician

At Beth Israel and Brigham and Women's hospitals, physicians, nurses, medical students, and other authorized clinicians gain access to the CCC clinical information system by going to any terminal (or personal computer serving as a terminal in the network) in the hospital, pressing the "Enter" key, and typing a confidential password. The CCC system offers clinicians the results of diagnostic studies, help in the day-to-day practice of medicine, help with decisions, and help with communication. Picture yourself once again as a patient in the hospital. Your doctor is on the staff of the hospital and has a password granting her (let me assume henceforth that your doctor is a woman) access to the clinical computing system.

THE COMPUTER AS A CLINICIAN'S ASSISTANT

Clinical information about you as a patient is retrieved through Patient Lookup, the most heavily used option in the CCC system. To use Patient Lookup, your doctor must first identify you by entering your name—or your medical record number, your financial number, your social security number, your room number, or the name of the nursing station nearest you, such as "coronary care unit." We have worked hard to make it easy for your doctor to find you. The computer adjusts for misspellings; our clinicians spell with admirable creativity.

Once your doctor has located you, the computer asks why she wants access to your electronic record, whether it is for clinical care, research, teaching, or administrative purposes. This information can then be helpful in evaluating the various ways in which the programs are used and the appropriateness of their use.

The computer then displays a list of options that can provide your doctor with needed information about you.

Demographic Information

If your doctor selects the Demographics/Discharge Diagnoses option, the computer displays your demographic information from the common registry; it then lists the names of the doctors who saw you for outpatient appointments, your visits to the emergency room, and your previous hospital admissions together with your diagnoses for each admission.

Results of Diagnostic Studies

The computer then displays a list of laboratories and departments from which your doctor can view the results of laboratory tests and clinical procedures. Suppose your doctor chooses All Labs—Most Recent Results. The computer will then display all your results for the past two days if you are an inpatient, or all results since your most recent admission or visit to a clinic if you are an outpatient. Information from the chemistry, hematology, and microbiology laboratories is available as soon as the diagnostic studies have been performed. Results are displayed in reverse chronological order, with the most recent results first.

If your doctor chooses Cardiology, Cytology, Neurophysiology, Radiology, or Surgical Pathology, the computer displays the examinations performed and a summary of the findings and their diagnostic interpretations; if she chooses Operating Room History/ Recovery Room, the computer displays your surgical procedures, either scheduled or already performed; if she chooses Blood Bank, the computer displays your blood type and associated antibodies, your transfusion history (including any adverse reactions), and an inventory of cross-matched blood (or autologous blood if you have previously donated) that is held in reserve and ready for her to use; and if she chooses Pharmacy, the computer offers her options to view the medications used during your hospitalization—either current medications or a summary for the present or most recent admission—and problems you might have had when taking your medications.

Most of this information is available from the terminals for up to a year; after that your information is removed from the active disk files but kept on magnetic tape for use if a retrospective analysis is needed.

Help in the Day-to-Day Practice of Medicine

The following options help your doctor with the daily routines of your care. The computers maintain a Personal Patient List—a list of the patients under her care. When you are admitted to the hospital, your name is automatically placed on your doctor's list.

With Edit Personal Patient List, your doctor and nurse can add or delete names from their lists. With View Hospitalized Patient List, your doctor can view the names of patients who are on her list and are currently in the hospital or have been seen by her that day in the emergency room. With Personal Patient Lookup, your doctor can step through the clinical data on each of her hospitalized or ambulatory patients without having to enter the names. This option can remind your doctor about laboratory tests that have been ordered. A Cross Coverage option permits your doctor, when she is temporarily off duty, to authorize others to look at data they may need to care for her patients. And at Beth Israel Hospital, a Discharge Summary program, developed by Daniel Sands and his colleagues in the CCC, helps your doctor coordinate each patient's clinical information for use at the time of discharge from the hospital.

The training programs for interns and residents in teaching hospitals are stressful, and these young doctors sometimes experience symptoms of anxiety and depression. At Beth Israel Hospital, an option called Confidential Counseling for House Staff gives the names, telephone numbers, and page numbers of clinicians in the Department of Psychiatry who are available to help interns and residents in distress (in the strictest of confidence). Further options permit your doctor to order tests and procedures, request delivery of your paper chart, and review the Medical Executive Committee's recommended preoperative evaluation procedures (as a check for good patient care before surgery).

A Universal Precautions option at Beth Israel Hospital offers your doctor a teaching program on safety measures when handling blood and other fluids from patients. Developed by Tamar Barlam and her colleagues in the infectious disease division, together with the CCC, this program is designed to help prevent untoward events, for example, an accidental needle stick, that could result in transmission of a viral infection such as AIDS or hepatitis. The program will also advise your doctor about the procedures to follow if an accident occurs.

With Notes, your doctor can type a message about your medical care for display whenever Personal Patient Lookup is used. These notes, which become part of your clinical record, can be used to remind her about specific problems, such as an adverse reaction to an antibiotic, or an allergy to a radiographic dye that is used in certain X-ray studies. Incomplete Medical Record informs your doctor about administrative chores that need to be done—discharge summaries that need to be dictated and medical records that need to be signed. (This is the least popular of the ancillary options.)

The Outpatient Setting

Charles Safran and his colleagues in the CCC and Health Care Associates at Beth Israel Hospital have developed programs designed to help clinicians in the outpatient setting. Among the many options now available to your physician and her colleagues is a program that will display her appointment schedule for the day. For each patient scheduled, the computer presents a list of past and current medical problems and an electronically stored narrative for each problem. The summary includes a list of the patient's medications and a list of appointments with other consulting physicians. This enables your doctor to refresh her memory and make plans for the future.

Nursing Options

Nurses are among the most frequent users of the many options in the CCC system. Some of these options, developed with Patricia Bourie, Radene Chapman, Peggy Reiley, and their colleagues at Beth Israel Hospital, were designed specifically for nurses to use in patient care.

These include Automated Nursing Assessment, which helps nurses assess the overall clinical situation of each patient, with specific nursing needs in mind; Bulletin Board, which displays standards of care and clinical guidelines; Dietary Orders, which allows nurses to request meals with specific clinical needs in mind; and Surgery Scheduling, which displays the operating room schedule and helps nurses get patients ready for surgery.

Utility Options

A set of Utility programs is also available to your doctor. One of them allows her to change her password in case of a suspected breach in security. An option labeled How To Use The Computer Terminal offers instructions for newcomers to the system and reminders for more experienced users. A Telephone Directory provides the phone number, beeper number, and room number of each member of the staff and of each department, as well as the weekly schedule of physicians in their specialty clinics. A Doctor's Office directory provides the address, phone number, and specialty (at Brigham and Women's Hospital) of each staff physician. This program helps interns and residents contact attending physicians whose offices are outside the hospital.

Help with Decisions

Also available at the two hospitals are programs designed to help your doctor provide you with better medical care as well as to help her or other doctors conduct research of potential benefit to patients in the future. Such programs are sometimes called "expert systems," but we prefer to refer to them as decision-support programs or computer-based consultation. Many such programs, developed with the technical support of Elaine Bianco and her coworkers, are in use at both hospitals. The following consultation programs are available to all authorized clinicians at Beth Israel Hospital.

ACID-BASE CONSULTATION. If your doctor needs help in deciding about intravenous fluids, there is an electrolyte and acid-base program that automatically obtains laboratory data such as your serum sodium concentration, serum creatinine concentration, and blood pH from the hospital's computer network. It then directs a dialogue in which your doctor supplies clinical information, such as your weight and any evidence of congestive heart failure. On the basis of the abnormalities detected, the program then asks further questions as needed to characterize the electrolyte and acid-base disturbances. Upon completion of the interchange, the program produces an evaluation note that resembles a consultant's discussion of the problem. The note includes a list of diagnostic possibilities, an explanation of the pathophysiology, recommendations for therapy, suggestions for additional laboratory studies, precautionary measures indicated by the illness or its treatment, and references to the medical literature. Originally developed by Howard Bleich in 1968, this was to my knowledge the first computing program to offer consultation on how best to treat a medical problem.

TREATING INFECTIOUS DISEASES. This program, which we call Bugman, provides your doctor with an interactive guide to the diagnosis and treatment of infectious diseases. Originally written in Converse by Michael Bookman, Bugman provides such information as the mechanism of action, route of excretion (such as the urine), and duration of effectiveness of antibiotics in the hospital's formulary. The program also lists the relative effectiveness of various antibiotics against various pathogenic bacteria, and provides dosage guidelines and cost comparisons for each antibiotic.

AN ON-LINE REFERENCE BOOK FOR MEDICATIONS. This program is an on-line version of the *Physicians' Desk Reference* (PDR). The book's indexes for generic name, brand name, product category, and company name have been merged. When your doctor enters the name of a medication, the program offers information about its pharmacology, the indications for its use, together with its side effects, interactions with other drugs, and dosage. Perhaps as a reflection of our times, clinicians have requested information about fluoxetine (Prozac), which is used for depression, more often than any other medication.

MEDICATIONS IN THE PHARMACY. Also written in Converse, Drugman is an interactive hospital formulary. The pharmacy maintains information about new drugs, new treatments such as calcium supplementation, and drugs being studied. Unlike the information in the on-line PDR, which is gathered from the manufacturer, the information in Drugman is gathered by a staff pharmacist in the hospital and reviewed by a senior staff physician before being released for viewing on your doctor's CCC terminal. Drugman contains data on indications for use,

FROM THE CYBERHERO COLLECTION...

BUGMAN

- ANALYZES EXCRETION ROUTES IN A SINGLE BYTE!
- LISTS ANTIBIOTIC EFFECTIVENESS FASTER THAN A SPEEDING BULLET!
- DOSAGE GUIDELINES MORE POWERFUL THAN A LOCOMOTIVE!

dosage, pharmacology, adverse drug reactions, and cost, and it compares medications in terms of cost-effectiveness.

MEDICATION CHARGES. This program uses the quantity of medication prescribed and information on each patient's insurance coverage to compute how much the patient will be charged for each medication received. This helps your doctor choose the least expensive medication from among those of the same quality.

A PROGRAM FOR PATIENTS WITH AIDS. HIV ProtoCall, also written in Converse, was developed in collaboration with the AIDS Clinical Trials Group of the hospital. It advises your doctor on the availability of experimental protocols for patients with HIV infection and on the care of patients taking experimental drugs. With HIV ProtoCall, your doctor can quickly learn whether her patients meet the criteria for inclusion in treatment protocols at any of the treatment centers in the Boston area.

JOGGING THE MEMORY ON-LINE. My father, a nuclear physicist, shared my concern about the exaggerated emphasis on memorization in medicine. He noticed that doctors seemed embarrassed when they had to look something up, whereas physical scientists would rely unabashedly on printed material for data and formulas, including their own. He thought it would be better for patients if doctors could come to grips with the imperfections of the human mind and rely more heavily on reference material and other reminders, even when they were confident of their information.

Fortunately, the excessive reliance on memory among physicians has begun to wane, and Clement McDonald and his colleagues at the University of Indiana deserve a sizable share of the credit. In a pioneering study, McDonald showed that errors in diagnosis and treatment could be significantly reduced when physicians were presented with computer-generated reminders, and that the impact of the reminders was independent of the level of the physician's training. Senior residents in his study benefitted as much from the reminders as did interns. In fact, the reminders had their greatest effect on a second-year resident, who had insisted at the beginning of the study that "what was needed was education of bad physicians about what they did not know, not reminders to good physicians [presumably including this resident] about what they knew."

Charles Safran, David Rind, and their coworkers in the CCC differentiate between an *alert,* which they define as a warning of a clinical event that needs immediate attention, and a *reminder,* which they define as an event that should be attended to in conjunction with the routine care of the patient. With the CCC system, the entire hospital and all its clinics and outpatient offices share one common database of patients. All the information from the laboratories and clinical departments for each patient is available to authorized clinicians on all the terminals. This enables your doctor to see alerts and reminders about a wide variety of medical issues whenever she signs on at a terminal.

ALERTS AND KIDNEY FUNCTION. A number of medications in current use are either excreted by the kidneys after acting therapeutically, or potentially toxic to the kidneys during their therapeutic action. If you are on a drug such as cimetidine (for peptic ulcers) that is excreted by the kidneys and your kidneys are not functioning properly, the level of the drug in your bloodstream may become unacceptably high. If you are taking a medication such as gentamicin (a powerful antibiotic), it may damage your kidneys. In either case, it would be wise for your doctor to consider reducing the dose or switching to a different drug.

The best laboratory measure of kidney function is the serum level of creatinine, a product of muscle metabolism that the kidneys normally excrete from the plasma into the urine. An abnormally high serum creatinine may indicate impaired kidney function.

At Beth Israel Hospital, if you are a hospitalized patient whose serum creatinine is high and you are taking either cimetidine or gentamicin (or a drug with similar effects on the kidneys), an alert goes out automatically from the computer to your doctor the next time she signs on to the computer. As another example, for patients with AIDS, an alert goes out automatically when it is time for an important diagnostic test or a change in treatment. Reminders, on the other hand, are invoked primarily in the outpatient setting. When your doctor signs on at the CCC system in anticipation of your visit, she is reminded of the timing of such important procedures as an influenza vaccination, a Pap test, or a tetanus shot.

ADDITIONAL HELP WITH DECISIONS. Also available under the decision support options at Beth Israel Hospital is a program developed by Daniel Sands that offers the solutions to a number of mathematical formulas. These are formulas that are used routinely in the care of very sick patients but that most clinicians do not know by heart. And in the outpatient setting, a program developed by Jonathan Einbinder and his colleagues in the CCC would advise your doctor on the use of anticoagulants to prevent the formation of blood clots. This may be necessary in patients with artificial heart valves or thrombophlebitis.

WITHDRAWAL OF THERAPY. This program offers guidelines for withdrawing or limiting the use of life-sustaining measures when death is close at hand and pain and suffering are to be avoided. The guidelines, which first and foremost respect the wishes of the patient and family but also conform to hospital policy and state laws, are available to help the clinician at any time of day or night from any of the terminals.

The Quest for Additional Information

When your doctor makes "rounds" in the hospital (meaning that she visits patients with interns, residents, and medical students), she tends to refer to two sources of information for help with problems that come up: the medical library and past clinical experience. "I think there was an article about this in the *New England Journal of Medicine*," and "I once saw a patient with a similar medical problem," are commonly heard comments along clinical corridors. Two programs conceived and developed by members of the CCC were designed to jog your doctor's memory and to help her to become better informed—PaperChase and ClinQuery.

SEARCHING THE MEDICAL LITERATURE. PaperChase, a bibliographic retrieval program, permits your doctor to search the National Library of Medicine's database of references to the medical literature. She can perform a search, read summaries, and—at a cost of $12 per article— order mailed photocopies of the full text. PaperChase provides access to over nine million references to articles in four thousand journals dating back to 1966. But more of PaperChase a little later.

SEARCHING THE CLINICAL DATABASE. Patterned after PaperChase and developed under the direction of Charles Safran, ClinQuery is a program on the CCC system that retrieves clinical information and enables clinicians and clinical investigators to search the computerized clinical data of all patients admitted to Beth Israel Hospital since 1984 (356,229 admissions through December 1996). Lists of patients based on demographic information; on results of diagnostic studies from the surgical pathology, cardiology, radiology, and clinical laboratories; and on blood transfusions, medications, and discharge diagnoses (from medicine, surgery, and all other clinical services) can be used to identify patients with attributes of particular interest.

ClinQuery has two primary uses: patient care and clinical research. If your doctor is deciding how best to care for you, she can use ClinQuery to look for a list of patients with a similar problem, and then examine each of these patients' medical records to look for treatments that might help you as well. If your doctor is doing research and has an interest, for example, in reasons for return visits to the emergency room, she can use ClinQuery to make lists of patients who have been seen in the emergency room and use the lists to explore alternative hypotheses. To protect patients' confidentiality, names and other personally identifying information are not displayed in conjunction with the lists of patients retrieved with ClinQuery.

Help with Communication

Electronic Mail, one of the first such communication systems to be installed in a clinical facility (at Beth Israel Hospital in the mid-1970s and at Brigham and Women's hospital in 1983), permits your doctor to send and receive messages from any of the terminals located throughout the hospitals and clinics. But more about e-mail later.

———

It is not sufficient for those of us working in the field of clinical computing to develop such systems, install them, and then proclaim success. Rather, it is incumbent on us to do our best to evaluate the impact of our efforts, for good or for bad, on the practice of medicine. All too often, programs purporting to do clinical computing are touted and marketed in the absence of evidence about their quality and usefulness. Questions such as "How often do the doctors use your system?" tend to go unanswered.

Let us turn, then, to the clinician on-line.

CHAPTER EIGHT

The Clinician On-Line

~~~

Ⅰt has been our working premise over the years that clinicians will be ardent users of computing systems if the systems are useful in the practice of medicine. If going on-line assists in the day-to-day activities of an arduous clinical practice, the doctor will go on-line early and often. If the computer makes it easier to get the results of diagnostic studies, if it helps with time-consuming administrative chores, if it offers good advice and consultation, if it offers ready access to the medical literature, and if it helps the doctor communicate with others in the field, these on-line services will be in great demand. But how do we go about testing this premise?

ASSESSING THE CLINICIAN'S USE

At Beth Israel and Brigham and Women's hospitals, we have done our best to evaluate the usefulness of the CCC system. We have tried to address the five questions of usage, cost, financial impact, popularity, and effect on quality:

· *How often does the voluntary user—the clinician who is under no obligation to do so—use the system?* There is no a priori reason for the clinician to use a computer unless it offers information that cannot be obtained as readily somewhere else. The results of diagnostic studies are typically available in printed reports; educational information and consultation can be obtained from books, journals, and personal communication; and many of the references to the medical literature can be found in a book from the National Library of Medicine, the *Index Medicus*. If a computer programmed to perform these functions is seldom used, it probably offers no advantage over traditional methods of processing and presenting this available information. Attention should then be directed to the program rather than the clinician.

•   *What is the cost of the system?* Is good clinical computing affordable?

•   *What is the effect of the system on the finances of the hospital or clinic?* Does the computing help out in the fiscal department?

•   *What is the attitude of the user toward the system?* Is the computing perceived to be helpful? Does the computing make life easier?

•   *What is the effect of the system on the quality of medical care?* This, of course is our reason for being.

Voluntary Use of the System

A distinguishing feature of the clinical computing systems at Beth Israel and Brigham and Women's hospitals is the intensity and extensiveness of their use, without coercion. Doctors, nurses, medical students, and other clinicians are heavy users of the CCC system. As they have learned that the programs are reliable and that the computers are almost never down, they have come to rely on the computing system for help in the care of patients. When the laboratory programs were first available at Beth Israel Hospital (before terminals were installed on nursing units), interns and residents discovered that they could see the results on terminals in the laboratories as soon as the tests had been performed. They descended from the nursing stations and commandeered the laboratory terminals, sometimes to the consternation of the technologists. In response to the demands of the house staff, terminals were installed on the nursing stations and used with increasing frequency. As I mentioned, there are now well over four thousand terminals in each of the hospitals and its supporting clinics.

Keeping Track of Use

The computer-assigned password that identifies each user and permits access to the CCC system also provides an electronic signature for each transaction with the computer. We have used these signatures to determine the frequency with which the computer programs are used by staff doctors, house officers, clinical fellows, nurses, medical students, and other clinicians in the two hospitals. The intensity of the use by these voluntary users can be taken as a measure of the system's helpfulness.

During the week of February 23 to 29, 1992, a total of 2,354 clinicians at Beth Israel Hospital—1,022 nurses, 523 health assistants, 305 interns and residents, 352 staff physicians, 103 clinical fellows, and 49 medical students—used one or more of the options in the clinical information system 69,784 times. The Patient Lookup option was the most heavily used. During that week, clinicians looked up data on hospitalized patients 34,614 times—a 172 percent increase over a comparable period in 1984, during the early days of the CCC system. During the same week, clinicians looked up clinical data on ambulatory patients 21,497 times—an increase of 426 percent since 1984. As would be expected in a teaching hospital, clinicians in training were the heaviest users of Patient Lookup, with a mean of 45 inquiries per intern and resident and 25 lookups per medical student.

Among the programs designed to help with decisions, PaperChase was used to perform 1,556 searches of the National Library of Medicine's database. Clinicians used the other decision-support programs a total of 1,288 times.

During the week of April 25 to May 1, 1994, the number of lookups of clinical information for inpatients was down to 30,264 in comparison with the comparable week in 1992. On the other hand, the number of lookups for outpatients was up to 27,023, an indication of the shift in American medicine to outpatient care. As I write, there are 3,674 clinicians with passwords to the CCC system at Beth Israel Hospital.

During the week of October 3 to 9, 1988, 2,262 clinicians at Brigham and Women's Hospital—549 physicians and 1,713 nurses, health assistants, and students—used one or more of the options in the clinical information system 89,101 times. As at Beth Israel Hospital, Patient Lookup was used most often: clinicians made inquires about 1,306 inpatients 40,998 times and about 5,402 outpatients 14,383 times, and physicians in training were the heaviest users. Among the 299 interns and residents who used the system during that week, the mean number of inquiries was 59.

During the same week in October 1988, clinicians used the consultation program on antibiotics 111 times and used PaperChase to perform 947 searches of the medical literature.

Since 1988, in conjunction with an increasing number of terminals and their ready accessibility, use at Brigham and Women's Hospital has continued to rise. As I write, the CCC system at Beth Israel and Brigham and Women's hospitals is among the most heavily used systems in the world.

Cost of the Clinical Computing Systems

Our surveys indicate that hospitals tend to spend 2 percent to 6 percent of their gross yearly income on computing, which is often limited to financial programs and patient registration, with perhaps a standalone laboratory system here or there, but all too often nothing much of use to the clinician. We have done our best to keep the costs of the computing systems as low as possible while providing computing that has the *primary purpose* of helping clinicians care for patients. During the developmental years, the total cost at Beth Israel Hospital was approximately 1.5 percent of the operating budget, and at Brigham and Women's Hospital, where financial programs were also included, the cost was approximately 2 percent of the operating budget.

Effect of the Clinical System on Finances

In keeping with the budgetary wisdom of high-priced consultants that permeates clinical facilities these days, most computing in hospitals and clinics begins and ends with the financial department. In our experience, however, and what we know of the experience of others, financial computing is not well suited to the clinical needs of the doctor and patient. It is difficult if not impossible to direct the large mainframe computer in the billing department to the needs of the clinician.

It makes more sense to start with a medical goal in mind for the computing—helping the doctor help the patient. In the first place, this is what medicine is all about. But in the second place, the finances of a clinical facility are better served when the financial computing is a *by-product* of the clinical system. The results of a diagnostic study, a red blood count, for example, represent more complex information than the amount to be charged for the study. It is easier for the computer to affix the charge to the study when the primary goal is to get the results to the doctor than to affix the study to the charge when the primary goal is to get the charge to the payer. And it results in better medicine and better financial accountability as well.

At Beth Israel, the time required to collect unpaid bills (the amount of money not yet collected divided by the mean amount of the charges added per day) dropped from sixty-five days in 1977, when the registration programs were first introduced, to thirty-nine days in 1982. At Brigham and Women's Hospital, the time required to collect unpaid bills was reduced from one hundred days in 1983 to fifty-nine days in 1988. Outstanding debts in the outpatient clinics were reduced by more than $6 million during a period when the cash collected from outpatient revenues increased by 45 percent.

Attitude of the User

In 1982, I wrote a computer-administered interview to find out how the clinicians at Beth Israel Hospital felt about the CCC system. Written in Converse, the interview asked the users to rate the computer's helpfulness, efficiency, and ease of use, and then requested comments and suggestions.

The interview was incorporated into the sign-on procedure; on entering a password, each qualified user was given the opportunity to answer the questions immediately, to defer them until a later date, or to avoid them altogether. Those who deferred were again invited to participate after a delay of at least twenty-four hours. Those who refused were asked to reconsider after a delay of at least a week. Those who refused twice were not asked again.

The results were gratifying. Of the 1,429 people invited to respond to the computer-based interview, 79 percent agreed, and both obligatory users (those whose jobs required them to work at terminals) and voluntary users (the clinicians who could have used more traditional means of communication if they so desired) praised the computing system. Of the 545 obligatory users, the majority indicated that the computer had made their work more accurate, easier, faster, and more interesting. Of the 586 clinicians who answered the questions, over 80 percent indicated that they used the computer terminals "most of the time" to look up laboratory results and found the computer terminals "very helpful" in doing so. Staff physicians, interns, residents, medical students, and nurses gave similar estimates for the helpfulness of the computer.

After the last question, users were asked to comment, if they wished, on their reaction to the computer; 133 clinicians, 23 percent of those who agreed to participate in the survey, took the time to type comments. Comments were almost always favorable. "The computer is one of the greatest assets of Beth Israel Hospital," wrote one enthusiastic intern. "I just find it more convenient (and fun!) to look up the lab results I need using the computer terminal," typed a nurse from one of the medical units. "When I was an intern here, we didn't have the computer system like this. If we had, I estimate that I would have saved myself an hour a day at least," commented a medical resident. "A computer [terminal] should be installed in the dialysis unit," typed a staff nephrologist—and we had one installed as quickly as possible.

Democracy and the Computer Interview

At the time of the survey, it occurred to me that Orwell's tyrannical Big Brother notwithstanding, the computer-based survey could actually be democratizing. One of the reasons for representational government is logistical: as a population grows, there comes a time when there are too many people to fit into a town hall. Lots of people can sit in front of interactive terminals, however, and computers are increasingly available—to people from all walks of life, both at work and at home. And the use of worldwide computing networks for interpersonal communication is flourishing. It seemed to me at the time that the computer could be used to empower people, offering them greater participation; with the computer, people could vote *on* issues rather than *for* representatives.

I would still argue that the computer-administered interview, used wisely and with care, is a valuable means of eliciting opinions about a wide variety of topics—in confidence and with anonymity if desired. And so it has been for users of the CCC system.

Effect of Computing on Quality of Care

The quality of medical care is, of course, our reason for being. It is also the most difficult process to measure. Difficult as this may be, however, it is still incumbent on those of us who work in the field of clinical computing, and those who market computing systems that purport to help in patient care, to face this issue head on and do our best to answer the question: Is the computer helping improve the quality of medical care? Is the computer helping the patient in matters of health and illness?

INDIRECT EVIDENCE. If it can be agreed that doctors for the most part engage in their diagnostic efforts with good reason and good will and with beneficial results for their patients, then the computing system that offers them the information they have requested, with more ease, speed, reliability, and accuracy than is otherwise possible, is improving the quality of care. The extensive, intensive voluntary use by clinicians at Beth Israel and Brigham and Women's hospitals is convincing, if indirect, evidence that computing is making things better for doctors and patients.

DIRECT EVIDENCE. Direct evidence is harder to come by. Our efforts to date have been with the alerts and reminders that are offered automatically to the appropriate doctors at the time they sign on to the CCC system. Consider, for example, a man who is taking gentamicin for an infection and has an abnormally high serum creatinine level, indicating that the gentamicin may be harming his kidneys as a toxic side effect. If an automatic alert about this situation leads the doctor to change the drug or reduce the dosage of gentamicin, the quality of medicine has been improved.

Under the direction of David Rind and Charles Safran, the CCC studied the effects of alerts and reminders on the practice of medicine. Doctors who received the alerts took substantially less time to change or discontinue kidney-related medications than did doctors who were not offered the alerts.

In a like manner, the time to act on clinical events, such as the need for a flu vaccine or referral for an eye exam, was substantially shorter when the doctor was reminded by the computing system of the need to act. Furthermore, the alerts and reminders have been well received by physicians as judged by their responses to a computer-conducted survey. We conclude that computer-delivered alerts and reminders beneficially affect physician behavior and thereby improve the quality of medical care.

THE TEACHING POWER
OF CLINICAL COMPUTING

In the tradition of John Dewey, who advocated "learning by doing," our clinical computing systems promote learning in the context of caring for real patients rather than in the isolation of the classroom. At any time of day or night, a physician in training at Beth Israel Hospital can look up information on the computer. Suppose that an intern caring for an elderly man is informed by the computer that his patient has low serum sodium and blood urea nitrogen concentrations and a chest X-ray film that shows enlarged lymph nodes at the base of one lung with fluid along the surface—findings suggestive of a lung cancer that is secreting a hormone normally secreted only by the pituitary gland. The intern can use the computer to get expert consultation on diagnosis and treatment (data from the laboratories and clinical departments are transferred to the consultation programs automatically), use ClinQuery to find information on other patients with these abnormalities, use PaperChase to search for related articles in the medical literature, and use electronic mail to communicate with other clinicians in the hospital. Physicians in training use our clinical computing system thousands of times each day, learning from the computer while helping in the practice of medicine.

COMPUTER-BASED
TELECOMMUNICATION

More and more medical information is available both to doctors and patients as a result of computer-based telecommunication. For the doctor, multiple Web sites and other means of access to the Internet offer a wide range of material. As one example, the Web site of the National Institutes of Health (http://www.nih.gov) offers NIH Clinical Alerts, which communicate the results of clinical trials as soon as they are available. In addition, clinicians can readily obtain current wisdom on the management of a broad range of common important medical problems, such as urinary incontinence, benign prostatic hyperplasia, early HIV infection, cancer pain, and low back pain. Most of this information is presented in a noninteractive manner, however. Much of what is available to clinicians on the Internet is also available in pamphlets, textbooks, and other medical publications; to date, few medical journals are transmitted in their entirety. And of course the doctor as user must consider the source of the literature and be wary of misinformation. But a very large amount of reading matter, much of it accurate and informative, is available over the Internet at any time of day or night, seven days a week, fifty-two weeks a year.

Telemedicine

I mention telemedicine here although it is beyond the scope of this book. Telemedicine is the name for the emerging field of remote medical consultation by two-way television. It allows the clinical expert to view pictures such as X-ray films or surgical pathology slides transmitted from remote regions with high resolution. The clinician who is caring for the patient can thus obtain the expert's advice and consultation on the spot, in real time. Still in its early stages, telemedicine is now mostly used to get help to doctors and nurses caring for patients in sparsely populated rural areas. Most of the work thus far with telemedicine has been in the field of radiology.

PaperChase

How does information of use to the clinician and patient find its way to the Internet? My favorite example is PaperChase, a program whose purpose was to give people the ability to search the medical literature. I am not a disinterested observer. The inventor of PaperChase, Howard Bleich, has been my colleague in clinical computing for over twenty-five years. But I consider PaperChase to be among the most important contributions to emerge from the field of clinical computing.

In 1966, the National Library of Medicine, a division of the National Institutes of Health, established Medline, an electronic database that would contain references to articles published in the world's best medical journals. For each article referenced, a medical librarian would enter into Medline the title, the authors, the journal (together with the page numbers, volume, and year of publication) and medical subject headings (MeSH terms), which are words assigned to help define the subject of an article. For example, "computers" is a MeSH term that would be assigned to an article about computers in medicine, even if the word "computer" did not appear in the title of the article. (The full text of articles is not part of Medline, because of the great amount of electronic storage this would require.)

Each month, twenty-five thousand new references are indexed and abstracted. Medline now has over nine million references to articles from over four thousand journals. Bringing together as it does the world's medical articles that have been published in accredited journals, Medline has been a powerful contribution from our federal government to the practice of medicine and to medical research.

As designed by the staff of the National Library of Medicine, Medline was to be used by highly trained medical librarians who were experienced with the complex programming language (ELHILL) that permitted them to use the computer to search for articles; and until 1979, users of Medline were required to consult with an experienced searcher, a librarian, who would serve as an intermediary and perform the desired searches. Such medical library resources were typically unavailable to patients and could be inconvenient, time-consuming, and expensive for clinicians and scientists—who would, after one or two tries, often revert to card catalogues and books such as the National Library's *Index Medicus* for help with their searches.

It was Howard's idea that people untrained as librarians and inexperienced with the use of computers could themselves search Medline to good purpose. This was a radical idea for its time, and not all medical librarians accepted it. But to their credit, the librarians on the granting agency of the National Library, even those with reservations about the project, put suspicion aside and voted to give Howard and his coworkers financial support to develop his program.

An Observational Experiment

On August 1, 1979, Howard installed PaperChase on a computer terminal in the Beth Israel Hospital library. Patrons of the library, most of whom had never used such a terminal before, were then free to use it at any time of day or night. No instructions were provided, no users' manual was written, no announcements were made, and no publicity was given. On the screen was a message that read: "PaperChase: a computer program to help you search the medical literature. To start the program, press the ENTER key." The program itself was designed to be self-instructional and to offer advice and suggestions on how best to proceed.

Between 4 P.M. and midnight, 12 people signed on and performed searches; the next day, 39 people signed on and performed 75 searches. During the first year, 1,229 people performed 10,678 searches—more computerized searches of the Medline database than were performed at any other institution in the country. During the third year, 2,202 people performed 16,803 searches. House officers were among the heaviest users.

Over the years, as the number of users grew, PaperChase was installed in the other Harvard teaching hospitals, and later in private offices and institutions throughout the United States and abroad. In the late 1980s, PaperChase was put on the Internet, and it now has its own Web site as well. On a typical weekday, there are now about 3,000 searches with PaperChase. Initially used primarily by clinicians and scientists, PaperChase is used increasingly by patients as well. Lawyers, administrators, and financial people are also among the growing ranks of those who seek access to the medical literature.

Since the inception of PaperChase, a number of commercially available products to search the medical literature have appeared on the market, and are available for use on the Internet as well as on stand-alone personal computers. And the National Library of Medicine now offers Grateful Med, its own general-purpose access to Medline.

ELECTRONIC MAIL FOR THE CLINICIAN

Electronic mail on the Internet—generally called e-mail—is heavily used these days by clinicians as well as patients. There are news groups and mailing lists primarily for clinicians in virtually every specialty, and numerous news groups and mailing lists are shared by clinicians and patients in the spirit of partnership, collegiality, and self-help.

Increasingly, also, physicians are proffering medical advice to people over the Internet. This raises interesting issues concerning malpractice liability. Among the doctors I know who are providing this service on an informal basis with no fees involved, there is a consensus that this is a humanitarian service rather than a medical legal transaction. There have been no lawsuits to date that I know of. Would that this will remain the case.

With our own e-mail systems in use at Beth Israel and Brigham and Women's hospitals, we have done observational studies that have given us some insights into the dynamics of this powerful new form of communication.

E-Mail in Two Teaching Hospitals

In 1976, when Howard Bleich and I and our many colleagues began to develop the clinical computing system, Bob Beckley and Saul Bloom developed an e-mail system to go with it, first at Beth Israel Hospital and then at Brigham and Women's. The idea was that e-mail would help the people in the admitting and medical records departments communicate with each other and with those of us in clinical computing who were working with them to develop and maintain their systems. None of us, however, realized that e-mail would revolutionize communication. As more and more programs were added, as more and more terminals were available, and as more and more people were signing on to use the programs in their day-to-day activities throughout the hospital and outpatient clinics, the number of users of e-mail and the extent of their use grew dramatically. E-mail was being pulled by those who wanted to use it; it was not being pushed by those who designed it, who were content to observe in amazement.

With our earliest version of e-mail, each user with a password could write and read messages to other password holders. Shortly thereafter, at the request of the users, we added the ability to send messages to individually compiled lists of people, to lists of members of one or more departments, or when deemed necessary, to all holders of passwords who were affiliated with the hospital. For example, an instructor in psychiatry could establish a list of his or her medical students and then use this option to forward advice to the group or invite them to a teaching session; each student, in turn, could acknowledge receipt of the advice, perhaps ask some questions, or indicate plans to attend. A chief resident in medicine could notify all residents that an instructive, unscheduled conference was about to occur, and a technologist in the blood bank could notify all who signed on that there was an urgent need for a particular type of blood.

Soon additional features were added. At the time of signing on, each user was informed about new mail and offered the opportunity to read it then or later. Users could send mail immediately or post it for future delivery. They could store mail that had been read in folders of their choice for future use; they could view messages previously sent, and reread their old mail; and they could edit messages received and then forward them to others.

We also incorporated two options that have been very helpful in our experience but are still not commonly part of other e-mail systems. Inquire If Message Read enables you to determine whether your message has been received. This is particularly helpful if you have not yet received a reply to a message of importance. Retract Mail enables you to retract a message if it has not yet been read and you have second thoughts about sending it or would like to make changes. With the retract option you can experience the psychological benefit of a verbal catharsis—after sending a note in anger, for example—without suffering the diplomatic consequences. Once the message has been read, of course, the proverbial die is cast. (The neurologist in me is looking for a way to retrieve the message *after* it has been read, but I have been unsuccessful to date.)

In some cases the computer itself now generates messages. When a patient is readmitted or seen in the emergency room, a message to that effect automatically goes to all physicians on whose Personal Patient List the patient's name appears. Physicians have told us that they very much appreciate this feature; it alerts them when one of their patients returns to the hospital, even if under the care of another physician, and it eliminates the need for them to telephone the emergency room repeatedly to find out whether an expected patient has arrived.

Assessing Use

Once again, we like to evaluate the e-mail system by how often it is used by voluntary users—those whose jobs do not require using it. And use has been extensive. During the week of February 23 to 29, 1992, a total of 2,354 clinicians at Beth Israel Hospital—1,022 nurses, 523 health assistants, 305 interns and residents, 352 staff physicians, 103 clinical fellows, and 49 medical students—sent about 20,000 pieces of e-mail. As of 1996, four years later, they were sending over 30,000 messages a week. Those who were most directly involved in patient care were the heaviest users. And at Brigham and Women's Hospital, where we installed a comparable e-mail system in 1983 as part of the CCC system there, use has been equally extensive.

During a computer-conducted survey at Beth Israel in 1992, 90 percent of those surveyed indicated that the e-mail system "made life easier" for them and 61 percent felt that e-mail had actually had a "humanizing influence" on their lives. Furthermore, many favorable comments about e-mail have come our way *by* e-mail. "This has been a very helpful service and has added to our ability to provide good care, [to] communicate . . . and has been a real time saver as well," wrote a staff physician in obstetrics and gynecology at Brigham and Women's Hospital.

Although most of the messages sent and received are related to patient care or other issues that pertain to work within a clinical facility, personal messages are common as well. At both hospitals, a rapidly growing number of people with specialized interests have developed electronic mailing lists for intercommunication. In these institutions, where the primary goal is the care of others, e-mail groups serve the purpose of self-care as well—an electronic form of group therapy, much like the mailing lists on the Internet.

The CCC e-mail system at Beth Israel Hospital is now connected to the Internet and can be used to send and receive messages on the Internet, as well as for intramural conversation.

A Special Niche for E-Mail

In the clinical situation, when you must reach someone in a hurry—when there is a medical emergency, for example, and you need to get in touch with a doctor immediately—the best form of telecommunication is the electronic "page," the beeper, or the portable cellular phone. When it is imperative that you talk with a person at the time of contact, there is still no substitute for the telephone. On the other hand, the telephone has its limitations. The person you are calling may be away from the phone, and you must then leave a message or take the time to call again. In turn, you may be away from the phone when the return call comes in, and you may continue in this mode, back and forth in a time-consuming process known as telephone tag. Furthermore, your call may arrive at an inopportune time, when the person you are calling is available but otherwise occupied, thus forcing a choice between inconvenience at the moment or telephone tag in the future. And of course you can't edit what you have said on the phone. You can apologize and restate, but you can't retract.

When delays in conversation are acceptable, when you can wait awhile between a message sent and a message received, e-mail fills what was heretofore a void in communication. With e-mail, you can read and write messages at your own convenience and with assurance of delivery. You can send a message at any time of day or night without worrying about interrupting the recipient, who in turn will read your message at a time of convenience, day or night. As many of the users of the CCC mail system have pointed out, telephone tag for them is a thing of the past.

With CCC e-mail you can take your time when composing, editing, and revising a message—and if the message has been sent but not read, you can retract it. In this manner, second thoughts about what you have said can be kept to a minimum. Furthermore, stored messages, both sent and received, can be kept as a permanent record of past conversations.

With e-mail, group discussions are easy to initiate. You can readily bring others into your conversation by amending, annotating, and forwarding messages without having to coordinate your schedules. People in groups can participate at their convenience. And e-mail can serve to promote common courtesy. In our experience, "Thank you" and "You're welcome" are easily (and therefore often) transmitted—and much appreciated.

Well-meaning voices of concern are sometimes raised about e-mail. Will it depersonalize conversation? Will it dehumanize interpersonal relationships? Will people stop talking to each other? It is helpful to remember, however, that e-mail is an adjunct to face-to-face communication, not a replacement. It permits conversation when face-to-face communication is impossible, and when the telephone is impractical. Carefully written e-mail messages can improve working conditions and interpersonal relationships as well.

Potential Problems with E-Mail

Not all is right with e-mail, of course. First of all, it takes at least two people to use it. If you send a message to someone who rarely reads e-mail, if your message falls on blind eyes, so to speak, the advantages are lost. However, where thousands of people are using the computer each day for a wide variety of purposes and where e-mail is one of many available options, as it is with the clinical computing systems at our two hospitals, e-mail becomes part of the routine and messages are read and written with high volume and consistent regularity. In our experience, it is the rare user who doesn't turn repeatedly to e-mail, day in and day out.

Second, there is the issue of unsolicited (read junk) e-mail. You may get more electronic messages than you care to read. There is these days what has been aptly called an information explosion. It has been estimated that there is more information available to the reader of one issue of the *New York Sunday Times* than was available to any literate person throughout the entire eighteenth century. Cognitive overload is of real concern to us these days as we attempt to sift and winnow the information that confronts us. It is imperative, therefore, that users of any e-mail system be able to dissociate themselves from mailing lists that yield unwanted material. Users should be able to search on-line for information they want and need, from the bulletin board to the interactive encyclopedia, but at the same time, they should be protected from masses of unsolicited materials that serve only to clutter the mind.

Third, there is the emotive aspect of e-mail. Just as we noticed years ago that people are sometimes more comfortable with a computer than they are with a doctor while answering questions of a potentially embarrassing nature, there is a tendency for some people to emote more freely by e-mail than they would in person. Sometimes the most mild-mannered, gentle person will let go at the computer with a tirade that would never occur face to face, like the humble pedestrian who becomes a hostile antagonist behind the wheel of a car. And sometimes people will send messages that are just plain ill advised, messages that may come back to haunt them.

Fourth, there is the issue of the attractive nuisance. Will people waste their time with e-mail? Will teleconverse supplant more useful human endeavors? Will it be used for mischief? In this regard, I would submit that e-mail is a neutral medium, which can be misused if people set out to do so. But rather than regulating its use—protecting people from themselves, as it were—I hope we can devote our energies to encouraging and reinforcing the gainful uses of this powerful new means of communication.

Finally, in spite of best intentions, there can be no certain protection of the confidentiality of any e-mail message in any system, although we have taken all the protective measures we can envision.

Having touched on the issue of confidentiality, I think it's time to pursue this essential issue further. How can we best protect privacy? How can we protect confidential clinical information once it has been placed in a computer?

ANNOUNCING THE ONLY FOOLPROOF,
GUARANTEED INDECIPHERABLE, ABSOLUTELY
CONFIDENTIAL HOSPITAL RECORDS
SECURITY SYSTEM:

DOCSCRIPT!

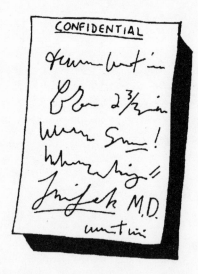

CHAPTER NINE

Confidentiality

J oe Louis once quipped about a forthcoming opponent, "He can run but he can't hide." Today the world is even more of a metaphorical ring, wherein we can run but we can't hide. Big Brother hovers over us, ready to descend at any time.

In days gone by, a man who was out of favor in his home town could pick up stakes and move to another community. There he could start anew, unencumbered by past transgressions or other best-forgotten aspects of his personal history; he could achieve geographic anonymity, if you will. When a person went west to the New World in the eighteenth century, or west to the Pacific in the nineteenth cen-tury, this was as much to escape the past as to find the future. Part of the American dream in those days was the chance to start fresh. Even the outlaw on the loose could find safe haven in a Hole in the Wall or a Teneke Springs. Now our pasts are with us for life, ready to be made public by interested parties if we don't take action to stop them. By "them" I mean those who would chip away at our Bill of Rights or stand by as others chip away, who would condone the use of technol-ogy, be it the telephone tap or the computer data bank, to intrude on our private lives, including our medical records.

Now if people want to find you and have the resources to do so, they can not only find you but find out all about you. Virtually anyone can get access to your social security number. (In Massachusetts, it's the number on your driver's license unless you take action to object.) On-line services on the Internet offer access to your demographic information (an on-line "White Pages" shows your house on a map). Banks, credit companies, testing companies, and the Internal Revenue Service obtain enough information as part of routine operations to compile financial, educational, and occupational biographies of us all. And this is not to mention how much information a reporter, a detective, or an FBI agent can obtain.

There is, of course, a gray zone between justified intrusion on behalf of the law and unjustified intrusion by a snoop or ideologue. This is part of the age-old conflict between the interests of society and the rights of the individual. But to paraphrase Samuel Johnson, the inability to distinguish dusk from dawn is not the inability to distinguish night from day. We know a snoop when we see one.

Those of us who believe strongly in the right to privacy must do our best to guard against unwarranted intrusion and fight back when it occurs. At the least we should speak out against the snoops and let *them* be the objects of public scrutiny.

THE MEDICAL RECORD

Just as no one can guarantee our privacy in other aspects of life, no one can guarantee the privacy of our medical records, whether they are on paper or in a computer. Once medical information is recorded in any form, it is subject to being divulged, despite the best intentions of the clinicians involved. The clinical transaction is not a simple relationship between patient and doctor. Even with a routine checkup, the receptionist knows the appointment has been made, the laboratory technologist knows the results of the blood test, the X-ray technologist knows how the film has been interpreted, and the pharmacist knows which medications have been prescribed. These people, as well as the doctor, may all be committed to the protection of privacy, but leaks can and do occur.

In the past, it seemed as though everyone *but* the patient had access to the medical record; the clinician, the hospital administrator, the insurance company, the lawyer, or the government could lay claim to it more easily than the patient. This situation is changing today.

More and more patients have access to their medical records, sometimes even with editing privileges—if not with the right to delete, at least with the right to correct and append.

Some people don't mind if their medical records are available to others. Individuals differ widely when it comes to the need for privacy. For one person, pregnancy may be a joyous event happily related to others; for another it is something to hide. And many patients suffer from the stigmas associated with some illnesses and most emotional problems. It would of course be better if there were no stigmas associated with illness. Perhaps we can see to it that illnesses no longer need to be kept secret. Perhaps the Thomas Eagletons of the future can seek help for depression and still run for vice president.

Patients do have some control over the information that goes *into* their medical records—you don't have to tell your doctor everything, and you can refuse to undergo diagnostic study. Still, to get help from a doctor or a policy from a life insurance company you may have to divulge information that you would prefer to keep private. In the best of circumstances all medical information should be considered confidential, known only to those with good reasons to know.

The conflict between the rights of the individual and the interests of the group is especially apparent in the area of infectious diseases and behavioral disorders, in which one person's problem can adversely affect another. When one sailor with smallpox was put ashore on the east coast of the Queen Charlotte Islands in 1860, the population in Haida villages there was decimated within a period of several years. In such cases, as with other social conflicts, we must turn to the law for guidance, though only with extreme caution. When, for example, are public disclosure and quarantine justified in the effort to safeguard society? Still, most of us would agree that when it comes to most decisions about divulging information to people who are not involved in patient care, the patient should be in charge.

There is a direct relationship between the usefulness of a medical record in the practice of medicine and its potential for unwarranted disclosure. The easier it is to retrieve the information in the record, the less secure it is from breaches of privacy. To put this another way, the more easily an authorized clinician can make good use of a patient's record, the more easily an unauthorized person can make bad use of it. With this fine line, too little protection of confidentiality will compromise your privacy as a patient, and too much will compromise the quality of your care.

The Paper Record

The traditional paper chart, when at its best in protecting confidentiality, is at its worst as a useful medical record. The best defense against unauthorized intrusion into the paper chart is the illegibility of the doctors' handwriting; I have trouble reading my own handwriting, not to mention that of my colleagues, and I am not alone in this. Coupled with illegibility is the traditional disorganization of the paper chart. Since there is usually no index or table of contents, whatever information *can* be read is still difficult to retrieve and use.

On the other hand, if the paper chart is legible and well organized, as it is in a few exceptional hospitals and clinics, it is also more vulnerable to breach of privacy. Virtually anyone with a white coat, a nametag, and an imposing facial expression can walk into a nursing station, pull a patient's chart from the rack, and read it without being questioned—as a *Boston Globe* reporter did some years ago in a local hospital. Even Nurse Ratched would hesitate to confront such an intruder. Doctors don't like to be questioned, and anyone with a white coat and a nametag might be a doctor.

The Computer-Stored Record

The ultimate confidential computer would be a computer with no output. Many doctors and nurses have seen computers in medicine that behave as if they had no output. These machines are sometimes advertised as if this lack of output were an advantage—"complex encryption prevents access by unauthorized users." If you can crack the "complex encryption," you find that it has been protecting very little of any use—a situation reminiscent of Dick Gregory's experience during the civil rights years: he waited and waited at the whites-only lunch counter, and when at long last the staff acknowledged him, they did not have anything he wanted. At the other end of the spectrum would be the computer with unlimited output, one that yielded anyone's medical record to anyone who requested it, which of course would be at least as unacceptable.

In any clinical facility that houses patients' medical records, three groups of people, in addition to the patient or a designated surrogate, may want access to a patient's record:

• *Those with no legitimate reason to see any part of any patient's record.* This group includes nonclinical personnel, visitors, and intruders.

• *Those whose jobs entail using a limited portion of the patient's record.* This group includes the receptionist who makes the patient's appointment, the laboratory technologist who needs the blood count but not the results of the gonorrhea culture, and the billing person who needs to know the charge for an HIV test but not the results. (The fact that this person knows that a patient has had an HIV test is a privacy issue in its own right.)

• *Those who need access to the entire records of the patients under their care but should not see the records of other patients.*

PROTECTING CONFIDENTIALITY WITHIN THE HOSPITAL

When the medical record is in the computer, it is incumbent on those responsible for the computing system to keep intrusion to a minimum while helping appropriate authorized clinicians find the information they need. With the clinical computing systems the CCC developed for Beth Israel and Brigham and Women's hospitals, we have done our best both to protect patient confidentiality and to enhance the quality of patient care.

Preventing Access by Intruders

Each authorized user of the computers at the two hospitals gains access to the clinical information system by means of a unique, computer-assigned, confidential password. Only a few people in supervisory positions can instruct the computer to issue a password. The computer does this because we have learned that people who choose their own passwords tend to use their initials or another sequence that is easy for them to remember, but also easy for someone else to guess. The computer constructs a password out of consonants (no vowels) to make it intentionally difficult to memorize, in case it is deliberately or inadvertently observed. Typically the user invents an acronym to help with recall. A user can ask the computer for a new password at any time, and will receive a new password every six months in any case.

All users are advised that a password is equivalent to a personal signature, and that under no circumstances should it be shared with anyone. The extensive use of electronic mail in the hospitals and clinics, for personal as well as job-related purposes, provides another incentive to keep our passwords to ourselves; when passwords are shared, the wrong people can read our e-mail.

The computers at the two hospitals maintain a dictionary of passwords and the names of their owners. If an unauthorized person repeatedly tries to use an illegal password, the terminal beeps the Morse code for "SOS" eighteen times and stops responding to its keyboard. It stays unusable until someone at the computer center releases the software lock. With the use of passwords, we are putting a higher priority on confidentiality than on patient care; the need to enter a password slows the clinician's access to needed information.

Restricting Access According to Need

Each password permits access only to programs appropriate for its owner, and then only from terminals appropriate for those programs. For example, a password assigned to a laboratory technologist permits access only to programs in that laboratory, and then only from terminals located there; a password assigned to a hematology technologist does not permit access to results from the microbiology laboratory.

Some passwords can be used only for looking at data, some can be used to enter and edit data, and some can be used to issue new passwords. After a user has completed a transaction such as scheduling an appointment, assigning a room, or correcting a patient's identifying information in the registry, the password must be entered as a personal signature—another incentive not to share it. The computer then records the date, the time, the name of the person who performed the transaction, the program used, and the location of the terminal.

Access by Authorized Clinicians

Only the doctors, nurses, and other clinicians who are participating directly in a patient's care, or those who are authorized to do clinical research with the informed consent of the patient, have a legitimate reason to gain access to a patient's computer-based medical record. It might seem reasonable, therefore, to restrict each clinician's access to patients who are known to be under his or her care. On the other hand, in an urgent situation, any clinician in the hospital might need to care for any patient. A doctor might be called away suddenly or otherwise unavailable, or an emergency might arise that would require all available clinical help.

Accordingly, we decided that the password of each authorized clinician would permit access to the clinical data of all patients in the hospital registry. In so doing, we have given a higher priority to the quality of a patient's care than to the protection of the patient's privacy. Any staff doctor could look up information in the medical record of a colleague or a celebrity without a legitimate reason to do so.

However, we have taken steps to make such intrusion unlikely. When a clinician first receives a password, he or she must sign a computer-generated document promising not to look at clinical information unnecessarily. In addition, whenever a clinician looks up a patient's data, the transaction is recorded in the computer and is, on request, made available to the patient or the patient's physician. Furthermore, if the patient is thought to be in need of special protection—is a hospital employee, a family member of a hospital employee, or a celebrity—the computer displays a reminder that is applicable to all patients:

> To protect each patient's confidentiality, only those who are responsible for a patient's care should use this option. We record the identity of each user of Patient Lookup and will give this information to the patient or the patient's physician upon request.

In addition, from time to time the computer selects a patient at random and transmits the same message. With this admonition, a potential unwarranted intrusion, particularly if it is innocent, can be averted.

All staff members of Beth Israel and Brigham and Women's hospitals are themselves potential patients in the hospitals and are therefore included in the common registry of patients in the computing systems. It can be argued that these people need special protection from unwarranted intrusion by fellow hospital workers. Accordingly, we have implemented as a utility in the computing systems an option labeled View Lookups Of Your Own File. This option, which is used several hundred times each week, enables any member of the staff to determine who has obtained access to his or her clinical record in the computer.

In the outpatient setting at Beth Israel Hospital, Jonathan Wald and his coworkers in the CCC added a feature whereby the author of an electronic note can designate it as "monitored." The author of a monitored note will receive an automatic message providing the name of each person who reads it, the date and time of the viewing, and the reason the person gives for looking at the note.

Loopholes Beyond Our Control

Our approach to confidentiality is based on physical protection—most computer terminals are located in supervised areas—and on the use of individual passwords. But we have also relied on personal accountability and trust, and this has proved to be justified. Known transgressions have been rare. Illegibility notwithstanding, we believe that computerized medical records can be better protected than paper charts. We are certain that they can be more helpful to clinicians.

Of more concern to me than the protection of confidentiality within the walls of a hospital is the protection of confidentiality once clinical information leaves the hospital. For purposes of reimbursement, hospitals and clinics are now required to send confidential clinical information, linked to charges, to a broad array of third-party payers—strangers, if you will, who are beyond the control of the hospital, doctor or patient. Are *they* to be trusted?

IN THE HANDS OF STRANGERS

Before the Second World War, the fee-for-service system was the predominant means of payment for medical care in this country. The doctor billed and the patient paid, often on the spot. Most doctors developed their own fee systems, which depended on the patient's ability to pay. Payment was not always monetary. Commodities that the patient could afford—the proverbial bag of potatoes, for example—were sometimes accepted in lieu of cash. If a patient couldn't pay at all, the doctor would write off the bill, a form of socialized medicine, one on one. (A practice called "professional courtesy" meant that doctors would not bill or pay each other.) Only people who were directly involved in a patient's care—the doctor, the nurse, perhaps the office receptionist, and when needed, the local pharmacist—were privy to the patient's diagnosis and treatment. Confidentiality was based on a clinical ethic, a pact between the doctor and patient.

When a patient needed hospitalization, hospitals billed on a fee-for-service basis. Housing within the hospital was a function of a patient's payment status: *private,* a room to oneself for well-to-do patients; *semi-private,* a room shared with a few others, for middle-income patients; and *charity,* a large open ward for patients who could not pay. The private hospital catered to the affluent. The charity hospital, typically large and city-supported, was the medical repository for the poor.

In teaching hospitals, whether private or public, charity patients were part of the educational process; medical students, interns, and residents were their primary physicians. Charity patients were used for instructional purposes in surgery and obstetrics as well as internal medicine, in return for free medical care. This was sometimes to the patient's advantage. What the medical student lacked in experience could be compensated for, at least in part, by careful devotion to the task. Furthermore, in good teaching hospitals, the interns supervised the students, the residents supervised the interns, and an experienced staff physician supervised the group and was available to provide direct patient care when needed. What was lost in comfort—multiple examinations day and night by multiple doctors in training—could be gained in comprehensiveness; with all the redundancy, it was unlikely that something important would be overlooked.

The large open charity wards were short on personal privacy. The curtains around the beds were flimsy, and confidential conversations were overheard by patients in adjacent beds and by their visitors. (Unfortunately loose talk among clinicians in corridors, stairways, and elevators is still a common source of breach of confidentiality.) On the other hand, there was a clear distinction between those who had legitimate reasons to look at a patient's chart and those who did not—that is, those who were responsible for a patient's care and those who were not. For the most part, confidential information for all hospitalized patients was kept within the walls of the hospital. Patients trusted the hospital to protect their privacy. Breaches of confidentiality, when they occurred, occurred inside the hospital.

But this is no longer the case. Since the advent of medical insurance, the walls of a hospital are no longer a protective barrier against loss of privacy. A third party has arrived on the scene, a party of strangers from outside the clinical sanctum. And *they* insist on having access to patients' medical records.

You Bet Your Health

Buying an insurance policy is a form of gambling. When you buy life insurance, the insurance company is betting you won't die within the term of the policy, but you are betting you will. When you buy automobile insurance, the insurance company is betting you won't have an accident, but you are betting you will. And when you buy medical insurance, the insurance company is betting you won't get sick, but you are betting you will. The game begins when you pay the premium (ante up) to the insurance company (the house); if you default on your premiums, the company keeps your money and you lose your policy. It is understood that the house usually wins; otherwise the game could not go on.

This is unusual gambling, to be sure; the incentives are perverse. When you're playing poker, you do everything you can to win (honestly, of course). When you're gambling on your health or life, by contrast, you don't try to win. But if you do win, you expect to get paid. As in other forms of gambling, cheating can occur and sometimes does. Insurance companies may delay or disallow payments for legitimate claims, and insured people need protection against this. On the other hand, insured people may make fraudulent claims, and insurance companies want protection against that. They want proof of what they are paying for.

With the evolution of medical insurance, clinicians and hospitals have found themselves constrained to give out confidential information from patients' medical records. The people who pay the bill are now the third party in the practice of medicine.

The Third Party

In the early days of medical insurance, during the 1940s and 1950s, the concept of a third-party payer was controversial, particularly within the medical profession. The concerns were not so much about privacy as about finance. The American Medical Association, as a union dutifully representing its physician members, was concerned that third-party payers would impose restrictions on fees. Group insurance programs such as the Kaiser Permanente Plan in California and the Health Insurance Plan in New York came under heavy criticism from the AMA, even to the point of organized boycotts.

With time, however, which brought rapidly rising medical costs and an increased demand for insurance coverage, medical insurance plans, both for individuals and for groups, became more and more available. And the number of private plans grew at a seemingly exponential rate. What were once a few tax-exempt programs, such as Blue Cross and Blue Shield, have now become a vast array of nonprofit and for-profit corporations. Even the federal government, despite opposition from the AMA and other forces of economic conservatism, became accepted as a principal player with the inception of Medicare in 1965. Universal coverage is now in demand, and third-party payers are more than ready to market their wares.

The new kid on the block, and in some instances already the bully, is the managed care company. Some for-profit, some tax-exempt, managed care companies now wield great power over health care delivery. Marketing its medical payment plan primarily to the employer who provides coverage for its employees, the managed care company can determine which clinicians are participants and what services are reimbursable. The managed care company wants to know what it's paying for. But further, by controlling the purse strings it is also managing the patient's care, at least indirectly. This is particularly evident in behavioral health where the treatment prescribed, even to the number of therapy sessions allowed, is dictated by the third-party payer.

All third-party payers have financial computers to help them out. In fact, their rapid growth has been to a large extent *because* of their computing facilities. Some insurance agencies and managed care companies market more than one plan. Massachusetts now has about three hundred medical coverage plans. Insurance buildings are going up at a rate rivaled only by banks. Hospitals and clinics are competing to provide services for the plans. Whatever else it may be, and by whatever name, medical insurance is big business in a sellers' market.

Managed care plans tend to reverse the financial incentives in the practice of medicine. In the days of fee-for-service payment, the more time spent, the more procedures done, and the longer the stay in the hospital, the higher the fee. As a result, too much was sometimes done and inefficiency was not discouraged. With managed care, the less time spent, the fewer procedures done, and the shorter the stay in the hospital, the higher the profits (or nonprofit profits) for the payer. In hospitals and clinics with managed care plans, the financial incentive is to stick to the practice plans prescribed by the managed care company; cost overruns are absorbed by the hospital.

Universal Coverage

Despite the problems inherent in all medical payment plans, there is general agreement these days that the United States and its people would be far better off if we could all have medical coverage, regardless of our finances. We should all be protected from financial ruin if a medical catastrophe strikes us or a family member. Those who would otherwise be unable to pay for their medical care should no longer be dependent on the beneficence of their doctors and hospital facilities.

Third-party payers foster consistency in payment among patients, regardless of their personal financial situation, so that the distinction now is between insured and uninsured patients rather than rich and poor. Large open wards, even in charity hospitals, have for the most part disappeared, a relic of the past. Insured patients can choose their own doctor (within the limits of their plan) and can insist that the role of "teaching patient" be shared by all patients alike.

Whether there should be many insurance houses, such as we have in the United States, or one house—the government—and whether we should ante up directly through premiums, or indirectly through our employers or government, are hotly contested issues. But there is general agreement that those who have medical coverage are better off than those who don't, and that we must find a way to cover everyone.

But we must also confront the issue of privacy. The third-party payer in medical care, in whatever form it may take, represents a breach in the traditional pact of confidentiality between doctor and patient.

Beyond the Clinical Sanctum

Most medical facilities ask each of their patients to sign a release form, which gives them permission to send a patient's medical information to whatever agency will be paying the bill. All third-party agencies require the patient's name and other personally identifying information, which they use to verify that there was in fact a clinical transaction. In addition, the agency insists on knowing the medical diagnosis (at the very least), which is typically transmitted in the form of an ICD–9 code (*International Classification of Diseases,* ninth revision).

Moreover, the information sent to the agency usually goes well beyond the medical diagnosis. Diagnostic and surgical procedures, laboratory tests performed, and medications prescribed are often included. The results of diagnostic studies are not usually provided, but the mere fact that a test *was done*—for AIDS, for example—can be highly revealing. The same is true with medications: if a man is taking AZT (zidovudine), it is not difficult to conclude that he has AIDS. Sometimes agencies will go so far as to require the details of a patient's diagnosis and treatment. For example, a managed care plan may insist on a detailed psychiatric history from the clinician before covering psychotherapy.

Role of the Computer

In hospitals and practices that rely on traditional paper records, a manual process is used to send information to insurance agencies—

a process that is arduous and often inaccurate. In medical facilities that use computing in routine patient care, such as Beth Israel and Brigham and Women's hospitals, the information is already available in electronic form. There is an irony here. Just as computer technology can make it easier to protect the privacy of patients within the walls of a hospital, so the technology makes it easier to breach their privacy outside these walls.

Trusting Strangers

The explicit purpose of placing confidential medical information in the hands of third-party payers is to enable them to verify the legitimacy of financial claims. Little is known, however, about how the agencies protect the confidentiality of clinical information. Who within *their* walls has access to private information once it is in their computers? Do they use passwords? What are their procedures for issuing passwords? Do they keep track of use? How do they control against errors? How do they ensure accuracy?

I telephoned a number of insurance agencies in Massachusetts but have been unable to get answers to these questions. The usual response is "We conform to the laws of the state of Massachusetts." When I ask "What laws?" they refer me to the state government. When I call the state government, I am referred back to the insurance agency.

We are faced with a conflict between two legitimate interests—the insurance agency's interest in protection against fraud and the patient's interest in privacy. So far the scales are tipped in favor of the insurance agencies.

From One Stranger to Another

Protection against fraud is understandable. But when confidential information is passed from one agency to another, without the explicit permission of the insured, a trust is broken. When a company that markets both medical insurance and life insurance disallows a person's life insurance policy on the basis of the information in his or her medical insurance record, the patient has reason to object. And when an insurance company disallows a person's life insurance policy on the basis of information obtained from *another* insurance company, the person has even more reason to object. Both these situations occur. It turns out that third-party payers routinely send confidential information in their computers to those of yet another agency.

The Medical Information Bureau is a tax-exempt corporation that stores medical information from approximately seven hundred member insurance agencies. Member agencies can query the Medical Information Bureau for information about their clients. As P. S. Entmacher notes, the bureau has reported that "safeguards are taken to assure confidentiality, and there is no linkage with other computer banks," but details on these safeguards are not provided. The medical information housed in the bureau is outside the control of the patient.

The Medical Information Bureau maintains a very low profile. Few people other than the member agencies even know of its existence. Few people, and I am not one of them, know how their information is used. Is it used to compile mailing lists? For marketing? For mischief? What are the safeguards for ensuring confidentiality? What are the safeguards for ensuring accuracy? We, the insured, are in the dark. Our privacy is beyond our control.

A PRESCRIPTION FOR PRIVACY

It is time to achieve a better balance between the interests of the third-party payer and the interests of the patient. A legislative approach comes first to mind. Should we not turn to the government, state or federal, to pass laws that protect our confidentiality, laws that impose restrictions on what can be done with clinical information once it is in the hands of strangers? Indeed, some laws have already been passed, and others are on the way. But wait. It could be true, as Thomas Jefferson observed, that when a law is introduced to solve one problem, two problems are created in its place. Who would enforce the laws? Would the laws spawn yet another government agency? Perhaps we would have an FCCMI, a Federal Commission on Confidential Medical Information—publicly funded, of course. Would its employees themselves need access to the confidential information? How else could they make certain that the insurance agencies were obeying the law?

I have another solution. Let's stop the problem at its source. *Let's stop sending confidential information to third-party payers.* We can develop a classification system that documents each clinical transaction, based on levels of severity of illness, but is free of clinical content. This would protect the third-party payer, within reason, as well as the privacy of the patient. I say "within reason" because there is no absolute protection against fraud. Transgressions may continue to occur, though probably with no greater frequency than now, but privacy will be protected.

There is no a priori reason for charges to be linked to clinical information in perpetuity. Charges can be separated from clinical content within the walls of hospitals, clinics, and offices. I am suggesting a standardized stratification system that would group charges, by a new coding scheme, on the basis of agreed-on costs for preventive, diagnostic, and therapeutic measures. These charge codes, identified by the patient's name but separated from their clinical antecedents, could then be sent on to the third-party payer. Provisions for internal and external (independent) review could be established to ensure the legitimacy of the initial link between charge and procedure. But no confidential information would be transmitted except under the direction of the patient or an authorized surrogate.

In managed care plans based on capitation, meaning that the insurer pays a fixed amount regardless of the care given individual patients, medical information should also be kept in the clinic. Although the managed care companies now insist on clinical information for each patient in the plan, the ICD-9 diagnostic code at a minimum, there is no good reason why they should need this. If the costs to the clinic are higher than the allocated amount, the managed care company will *not* make up the difference. Accordingly, the company has no legitimate need to know how the clinic is spending its allocated funds on medical care for each patient.

There is potential risk to the patient, however. When budgets are thus restricted, the financial incentive is to have more patients but do less for each patient seen. The clinician is under pressure to cut corners; efficiency sometimes takes precedence over quality. When capitation is implemented, therefore, there should be provision for peer review to ensure a high quality of medical care. It is also imperative for the funds from the third-party payer to be sufficient to cover reasonable medical costs, and for funds to be held in reserve in the event of emergencies. But confidentiality could be protected with such a plan.

The Nay Sayers

The third-party payers will ask how they can trust hospitals and clinicians to give accurate accounting. They will argue that they are paying the bills and have a right to know what they are paying for. But we can remind them that they are being paid to pay the bills, and they are making a profit in doing so. Let us remember that until now the trust has gone in one direction, toward the insurance agencies. It is time for them to give their trust in return.

They might ask who will authorize the use of services; who will approve the plan for patient care. My answer is straightforward. When it comes to the managed care agency practicing medicine, my prescription is to *disallow it*. The managed care agents do not need to know the clinical information associated with charges for an individual patient. As things stand now, the financial conflict of interest and the trust that goes with it are heavily weighted in favor of the third-party payer. Let us reverse the process. Let us return the trust to the patient and clinician. Let auditing be done by a small group of disinterested peers, who would serve with the consent of all parties involved.

Third-party payers might argue that I am indulging in what some have called the leisure of the theory class. Clearly, there will be hurdles along the way, and the details of my plans have yet to be worked out. But think of the advantages. Privacy would be protected. No legislation would be needed. There would be fewer data to process, and money would be saved—by the clinics and taxpayers, if not the third-party payers. And we would not have to investigate the Medical Insurance Bureau. It would disappear on its own, with disuse atrophy.

PART THREE

Modern Times

CHAPTER TEN

Barriers to Clinical Computing

I f the computer is to become more widely available and useful as a patient's assistant—helping patients and their families maintain better health, manage medical problems when they occur, seek and use health care facilities in an enlightened manner, and participate as partners with clinicians in medical decisions—good materials must be written and tested. They must then be made available for use both on stand-alone personal computers and on networks such as the Internet. And progress is being made. Already there are good programs on PCs, for example those developed by David Gustafson, Patricia Brennan, and their coworkers to help patients with problems such as breast cancer or AIDS and by Lawrence Van Cura to help people assess various risks to their health. The rate-limiting enzyme in the development of these programs, to use a biological metaphor, is one of resources. Well-written, informative, interactive medical materials are difficult and expensive to prepare, and the question is how best to support their development. Fortunately, however, there are few administrative barriers in the way of progress. The barriers are primarily economic, and these can be overcome with pressure from the patient in the role of consumer.

Good computing for the doctor in the hospital is another matter. There is much hype about this, but prophecy is substituting for accomplishment. Ironically there is often more useful computing for the doctor outside the hospital, on the Internet. Why are there so many American hospitals, clinics, and private offices with little or no computing that helps the doctor care for patients? There are real and imaginary reasons. Let us consider the imaginary reasons first.

IMAGINARY BARRIERS TO CLINICAL COMPUTING

There is a tendency to assume that to introduce a computer to medicine is to introduce new, important clinical information that clinicians *should* acquire, and to assume that whether clinicians do so is a measure of their willingness and ability to master new technology. When terminals go unused, the explanation is sought in characteristics of the user, such as age, computer phobia, or lack of computer literacy, rather than characteristics of the computer programs, such as how well they work to help the clinician or patient.

Age and Computer Phobia

Blaming the already beleaguered clinician for being too old or computer phobic is a handy approach for computer manufacturers, systems analysts, and program developers whose programs are disliked and little used. It is reminiscent of the way automobile manufacturers used to blame drivers rather than defects in their cars—until Ralph Nader set the record straight with *Unsafe at Any Speed*. When computer manufacturers ask, "How can we get physicians to use computers?" they are more likely to mean, "How can we get physicians to buy computers?" A better question would be, "How can we make our computers helpful?"

In my experience, age and computer phobia are unimportant as deterrents to the use of clinical computing. In an informal study at Beth Israel Hospital in 1982, well before the widespread proliferation of personal computers, staff physicians—who were older and presumably more prone to computer phobia than the medical students and house staff—were nevertheless equally well disposed toward the clinical computing system and its helpfulness in patient care.

The same can be said for the population in general. With the advent of the Internet, millions of people are going on-line, undeterred by age or computer phobia. Computer phobia disappears rapidly when the machine is easy to use and helpful; and it has been amply demonstrated that people from three to ninety-three can use computers to their advantage.

Computer Literacy

Nor is lack of computer literacy an important barrier. People catch on quickly once they are able to try their hand. They don't need to know the inner workings of a machine to use it with good purpose. The belief that they do is an all-too-common misconception.

For the most part it is true that the person who invents a machine and understands its inner workings is also its first user. The early automobiles—Nicholas Joseph Cugnot's steam vehicle of the 1760s and Karl Benz's gasoline-powered carriage of the 1880s—were first operated by those who designed and built them. Almost certainly, Blaise Pascal was the first to use his mechanical adding machine (in the 1640s), Gottfried Leibniz the first to use his four-function mechanical calculator (in the 1670s), and William Burroughs the first to use his business machine (in the 1890s). Had Charles Babbage ever completed his digital computer (in the 1820s), he would for sure have been the only person who knew how to use it. And so it has been with the more modern vacuum-tube and solid-state machines, with programming languages, and with the software programs themselves.

Once a machine is in general use, however, it is no longer necessary for the user to understand its inner workings. Most of us drive our automobiles without knowing the theoretical foundations of the internal combustion engine; most of us use our telephones without understanding information theory, and turn on our electric lights without Ohm's law in mind.

So it has been with clinical computing. During the first two decades of the use of computers in medicine (the 1950s and 1960s), doctors who wanted to use a computer typically had to program it themselves, often in machine language. Programming in machine language (with instructions that are executed directly by the computer, one by one, without first being interpreted or compiled into simpler units) entails some understanding of the machine's inner workings. In the 1970s, most doctors who used computers were still doing their own programming. They had higher-level languages (compilers and interpreters) and programming was easier for them, but they were still in close touch with the machine.

Now, of course, things have changed. Clinicians who know nothing about the inner workings of their computers can, to good advantage, use programs written by others. With a few simple keystrokes (though as yet in relatively few institutions), they can look up the results of diagnostic studies, get advice on patient care, search the medical literature, and communicate with each other by electronic mail. Personal computers provide word processing and spreadsheet accounting programs that require little more understanding of the machine than how to turn it on. And of course, doctors and patients are using the Internet with increasing regularity.

Still, the idea that the doctor (or anyone else) must know the theoretical underpinnings of the computer—must be "computer literate"—to use the machine lingers on. This notion is kept alive in part by well-meaning, influential medical school academics, typically nonusers themselves, who are inappropriately embarrassed by their own inexperience with computers and who believe, misguidedly, that an in-depth knowledge of computational theory is a prerequisite for productive use.

Then there are those persistent professors, often erstwhile programmers themselves, who want a computer course (required) to be part of the medical school curriculum. They want their students to be computer literate. They forget that most undergraduates are heavy users of programs such as word processing (if not on their own machines, on machines provided by their colleges or universities) before they ever get to medical school, and that many doctors (particularly nonacademics) who have never taken a course in computing use personal computers to good advantage without worrying about computer literacy.

If a medical student *wants* to know the theory behind a machine (be it a computer or an autoanalyzer), there should be facilities within the school to encourage this. But when curricula are already full, when even clinical courses such as pediatrics and obstetrics are themselves sometimes electives, the argument for a required course in computing is unconvincing. Neither clinicians nor patients need be computer literate, in the sense of understanding the inner workings of the machine, to use the computer in the practice of medicine.

Turn with me then, if you will, to some of the real obstacles that keep computers from serving the medical community effectively.

REAL BARRIERS TO CLINICAL COMPUTING

With computing for the clinician, the forces of bureaucracy play a prominent role. The impediment to good computing is more managerial, administrative, political, and territorial than technical or medical. And doctors are partly responsible. In the early days of the computer, they suspected that the machines would encroach on the practice of medicine rather than enhance it. By the time they understood that computers would not destroy the art of medicine, the opportunity to influence the computing in their hospitals and clinics was largely out of their hands.

The Administrator

There are two types of librarian in my experience: the one who wants you to take out books and the one who doesn't. The former welcomes signs of use, signs that you have read and enjoyed a book. The latter worries that you might tear the pages, get food on the cover, or break the binding. The administrative goals of the institution determine which librarian will prevail. If the primary goal is to promote usage, it will be the former. If the primary goal is to protect inventory, it will be the latter.

In a like manner, there are two types of hospital administrator: the one who is both willing and able to help clinicians care for patients and the one who isn't. The former wants to make it as easy as possible for clinicians to practice good medicine, wants to say yes to requests for help, even when this entails flexibility, ingenuity, and conscience. The latter is much more comfortable saying no. (Flexibility, ingenuity, and conscience are administratively risky.) Which administrator will prevail is again determined by goals. If the primary goal is to promote patient care, it will be Type 1; if the primary goal is to protect administrative order, it will be Type 2.

My first real-time experience with hospital bureaucracy was back in 1962 at Clark Air Force Base in the Philippines, where I served as a neurologist for two years. During medical school, internship, and residency, I had been isolated from hospital administrators, who were few in number in those days (typically *one* vice president per teaching hospital, if you can believe it). But at Clark Hospital—a group of M*A*S*H-like Quonset huts—it was different. Medical Service Corps officers—the forerunners of the vice-presidential administrators and middle managers that now pervade American hospitals—were all about us. And for the most part they were Type 2 administrators—functionaries with neither imagination nor conscience (as Abba Eban once described the tax collectors of Mesopotamia). They would get to the hospital at nine in the morning, leave promptly at five, and dress in proper uniform, but whatever role they played in patient care served for the most part to *impede* the process.

An Administrative Formula

Not all administrators at Clark were Type 2, mind you. There were some Type 1 administrators who really wanted to help, but they were in the minority. Also, they were of lower rank—typically lieutenants or sergeants. For example, my staff sergeant—Sgt. Rulebender—could really get things done. In fact, the doctors there, who were very busy (the Vietnam War was escalating) and doing their best to practice good medicine, noticed an interesting phenomenon among the administrators: the higher their rank, the lower their competence (that is, their ability and willingness to help). With homage to C. Northcote Parkinson, I formalized this as an inverse proportion:

$$C \text{ (COMPETENCE)} = 1/R \text{ (RANK)}$$

This is not to be confused with the "Peter principle," which pertains to people who continue to be promoted because they are competent until they reach a position in which they are incompetent, where they then remain. The dynamics of $C = 1/R$ were to become increasingly clear to me as I learned about the process of military promotion.

At the end of each two-year period, the Medical Service Corps officer would receive what was called an "efficiency rating"—on a scale of "poor" to "outstanding"—from his (they were all men) superior officer, who was another administrator. Accordingly, the administrator's allegiance belonged to the administrator who would rate him, not to the doctors, whom he could displease without risk. Because it is virtually impossible to make a good suggestion without implying a criticism—why didn't the superior officer think of it himself?—suggestions were not well received. Hence, the fewer the suggestions about how to help the doctors and their patients, the higher the efficiency rating. And promotion depended on a rating of "outstanding." Accordingly, as the administrator rose in rank he became decreasingly willing and able himself and increasingly threatened by suggestions from subordinates (which in turn dampened their enthusiasm for making any). By the time the administrator made bird colonel, the process was complete: He was now a functionary with neither imagination nor conscience.

C = 1/R in Civilian Life

My career in the military ended after the usual two-year stint, but I have no reason to believe that C = 1/R is less apt today than it was in the 1960s. And I know for sure that it applies increasingly well to civilian hospitals—with their corporate ranking systems, such as manager, director, assistant vice president, vice president, chief operating officer (COO), and chief executive officer (CEO)—where Type 2 administrators are proliferating. They are hired, promoted, and fired by other administrators, to whom they give their allegiance. Hence, there is little administrative incentive for them to help the doctors. Type 2s are assisted in their pursuit of administrative orderliness by the currently popular view (promulgated by a surprising number of business schools) that the less the administrator knows about what he or she manages, the better will be the management. (Imagine a Type 2 administrator in the role of "vice president for *clinical services*"! Next hospital, please.)

The Type 2 gives much more importance, much more status to managerial position than to technical competence. Competence is high-risk for the Type 2, something to be kept in check—"No creative people in the inner office, thank you." The Type 2 is uncomfortable in the presence of people with tangible skills, such as the computer programmer, the engineer, the scientist, and the clinician (the clinician is a necessary evil at best in the Type 2 mind-set—"if only they could be done away with, but then . . . "). Only managers are welcome in Type 2 meetings. Albert Einstein would never get promoted in the Type 2 environment.

There are still some exceptional hospitals in the United States where Type 1 administrators predominate, and I have been fortunate to work in them and with the Type 1 administrators in the CCC. But I am afraid I must say their numbers are on the wane. The current trend toward the corporatizing of the American hospital can only accentuate the process.

It should be pointed out that competence in my equation is defined from the perspective of the clinician, not the administrator; surely, there are Type 2 administrators who believe that their process of

promotion is based on merit. The promotion of the Type 2 administrator, therefore, should not be confused with the well-known situation—the reverse of the Peter principle if you will—in which an
incompetent civil servant, who cannot be fired, is promoted as a
means of good riddance. Nor should it be confused with the "Dilbert
principle," whereby the administrator is promoted to a position of
harmlessness. The Type 2 administrator is not harmless.

Clinical programs are still not high among the priorities of Type 2
CFOs and CIOs, who control the computer rooms in most of our hospitals and clinics. If the financial computing systems get the bills out
more or less on time, their jobs are secure, and the board of directors
is pleased.

The Consultant

The consultant is endemic in medicine. Hospitals and clinics are big
business for consultants; CEOs and CFOs like to walk in their company. Just as Dylan Thomas's uncles were always present at Christmas
in Wales, consultants are always present in medical facilities. Consultants are particularly prevalent in medical computing centers; and they
are always in evidence at conferences on medical computing, wher-
ever they may occur.

Just as there are two types of administrator, there are two types of
consultant. There is the Type 1, who is knowledgeable and offers
forthright constructive criticism and useful strategies, even if the advice is unpleasant for the person paying the bill. The Type 1 is eager
to get the job done and move on to other challenges.

By contrast, the Type 2 consultant, who is typically paid by the day
(as opposed to the job), has a basic strategy: find out whatever it is the
person who is paying you wants to hear and then take as long as you
possibly can to say it. The replicating powers of the Type 2 are much
superior to those of the Type 1.

Typically, the Type 2 consultant has had little or no direct experience with clinical computing. Therefore, another strategy is to find
people in the client's institution who are *real* experts and who would
otherwise charge for their time, but who are obligated to spend time
with the consultant by administrative decree from "top management"
(read "Type 2 administrator"). Thus, while being lucratively remu-
nerated, the consultant can soak up some of their expertise to market

to future clients—learning on the job at the client's expense. A good deal, if you can get away with it.

The consultant's final report is glossy and replete with the current pseudospeak: "best of breed," "legacy systems," "data warehouse," "open systems," "connectivity," "client server," "interface engine," and "leverage." In the tradition of corporate parsimony, the report is prepared in boilerplate, designed for use in virtually *any* client hospital; only the names need be changed. And the report can be expected to recommend an administratively safe decision with no surprises (the good parasite does not destroy the host): perhaps some "downsizing" (from among the technically competent who also speak their minds), some "upsizing" (there is always a need for more Type 2s), and the purchase of computing from a large, well-known company whose product is mostly fiscal in function. It is important that the computing be at once expensive to buy, hard to install, and cumbersome to operate. This ensures the need for additional consultation in the near future, which is part of the recommendation.

The Type 2 consultant also serves as the flak catcher. The CEO, COO, CFO, CIO, and Mr. Binary can blame the consultant when things eventually go wrong. This protects their jobs and is of little consequence to the consultant, who—with the timing of the good snake oil salesman— has already left town. Only the clinicians and their patients are left to suffer; there will be no computing for them in the near future.

The Committee

As it is with the administrator and the consultant, so it is with the committee. There is the Type 1 committee, with a well-defined goal, a few members, and a short life span—a committee whose work is judged by outcome. And there is the Type 2 committee, with an ill-defined goal, a lot of members, and an infinite life span, whose work is judged by form and process.

Committees are at the foundation of most institutions, whether they are academic, medical, industrial, or governmental. All colleges and universities, for example, must have at least two of them: the admissions committee for students and the promotions committee for faculty. But I doubt that there has ever been an institution of any size with only two committees on its premises. The reason is that the committee is self-propagating; like Parkinson's "officials" or Type 2 administrators—who proliferate exponentially, regardless of the job to be done—the committee assumes a reproductive life of its own.

The explanation for this phenomenon, though perhaps not immediately apparent, is straightforward: it is more prestigious to form a committee than to serve on one. The most prestigious committee-related behavior, typically reserved for the president, governor, chancellor, or CEO, is to form a committee but attend no meetings—"the CEO's Standing Committee on Management Information Systems," for example, reminiscent of Her Majesty's Ship, which she never boards.

A somewhat less prestigious move, typically reserved for the CFO or an administrator of equivalent rank, is to form a standing or primary committee, put in a perfunctory appearance, tell the members about the great importance of their mission, and then disappear to be seen no more. But what about those who must actually serve on a committee and attend its meetings?

For those who must serve, the best role by far is that of chair, one of whom was the now-forgotten genius who, in the primordial era of the institution, conceived of a way to keep his committee meetings to a minimum and enhance his prestige: he invented the subcommittee—and formed two of them. It's important that there be at least two subcommittees. A single subcommittee might resemble the primary committee and be confused with it, undermining the committee chair's prestige rather than enhancing it. The newly appointed chairs of the two subcommittees each move quickly to form two of their own—sub-subcommittees. Imagine a rising pyramid of committees, proliferating in a manner independent of whatever ostensible purpose the primary committee was supposed to serve.

It should be mentioned here that I know people in a number of institutions (and it is likely that you do as well) who actually *like* to go to meetings, who welcome the opportunity to serve on committees or subcommittees at any level, and who always respond to the chair's closing question—"Is there any other issue to discuss?"—with another issue. These people, of course, augment the proliferation of committees and their progeny. But for those who don't like committees yet must serve on them (their jobs may depend on it), here are a few tips that may prove useful: (1) Avoid subcommittees at all costs. (2) Never accept a writing assignment. More than likely, the assignment is a gambit to transfer responsibility (read "onus") to your shoulders. Now the chair will be waiting for you; *you* will be the one who is slowing things down. If you pass the chair in the hall, you will feel guilty; if things go wrong, it will be your fault. And whatever you finally do write will go unread, laid to rest in the filing cabinet of the person who formed the committee. (If it is bulk that is needed, offer to clear your desk.) (3) Fortify yourself with a self-beeper for use when there is no hope of an early closure. And (4) skip one meeting. If there are no repercussions, try a sliding-scale approach; first (at random) skip a meeting a month, next (judiciously) skip two meetings a month, then (with caution) three, and finally (de facto) resign. You may never be missed. Now maybe you can get some work done.

Type 2 committees, subcommittees, and sub-subcommittees are pervading hospitals and clinics at an alarming rate. With the Type 2 CFO or CIO in charge of committee proliferation, the committee is yet another formidable barrier to good clinical computing. The more committees there are, the more meetings to attend. When you are always in a meeting, it's hard to find time to do much computing.

The Company

Vendors of hospital information systems usually try to sell their products to a CFO or CIO (and resident consultant), to one of the hospital's vice presidents, or to a departmental director—*not* to a clinician. Accordingly, the programs sold and delivered are financial, managerial, or stand-alone departmental; they may serve the needs of the buyer or department but are of little use to the clinician in practice.

Unfortunately, information about the use of computing by clinicians is hard to come by. Data from companies that market computing systems are often unavailable or unreliable. Some time ago I saw a press release claiming that one hospital was using a commercial system with "more than 250 working stations, . . . making it one of the world's largest patient data management systems." A telephone call to the hospital revealed that most of the workstations had yet to be installed, and not one was in use.

The Cost

In the early days, capital investment in hardware was a major consideration in any decision about the type of computing a hospital or clinic would have. If the hospital had already purchased a large, expensive mainframe computer for fiscal purposes, then clinical programs, if they were to be implemented, were expected to run on the same machine, even though it was not well suited to these programs. This is no longer the case. Many hospitals and clinics can now afford to replace their overpriced, cumbersome mainframes with networks of inexpensive and flexible minicomputers. They can, that is, if the forces of bureaucracy can be overcome.

REINVENTING REORGANIZATION (A PARABLE FOR MODERN TIMES)

I was to learn that [managers] tend to meet any new situation by reorganizing, and the wonderful method it can be for creating the illusion of progress while producing confusion, inefficiency, and demoralization.

—*attributed to Petronius Arbiter, 66 A.D.*

In the beginning, physicians were wary of computers. They were more than willing to leave the big machines alone, out of sight in the fiscal department, safely removed from the practice of medicine. By the time physicians realized that computers might actually help with patient care, territorial imperatives had been firmly established: the CFO and his colleague, Mr. Binary, had control of the computer and of the large budget needed to support it and were not about to give these up. Like office space and parking, the computer had become an important source of managerial control.

In most American hospitals and clinics, the CFO and Mr. Binary continued to control the computer room (as they still do today), and clinical programs were not high on their list of priorities. In one hospital, however, things were different. Mr. Rulebender, now out of the Air Force, was director of the computing center at Metropolitan Hospital. Working closely with his clinical colleagues and a talented group of computer programmers and engineers, he had developed a network of minicomputers, which were working well from the clinicians' perspective, with programs (developed in-house) that delivered the results of laboratory studies to doctors, nurses, and students on the floors and in their offices, in a manner that was easy for them to use. The doctors and nurses sent love letters to the computer by electronic mail. The financial programs ran as a by-product of the clinical systems, and the hospital's receivables were in good shape.

Then there was a change in management. Mr. Rulebender now reported to the CFO, newly arrived. (There was as yet no CIO.) The CFO didn't like Mr. Rulebender—he was not a company man; he did not believe in organizational charts; he allocated too much of the hospital's computing to the doctors (the CFO didn't like doctors, either); he didn't understand that computing should be governed by financial needs, not patient care; he didn't show the proper respect; and his irreverent attitude was hardly amusing. The CFO couldn't say these things out loud, of course. "Rulebender can't manage," was the best he could do.

In accordance with one of Parkinson's laws ("An official wants to multiply subordinates, not rivals"), the CFO hired two subordinates, one of them Mr. Martinet, who had become a computer consultant after leaving the military as a full colonel. Martinet, now COO, didn't like Rulebender either (for the same reasons), but much to his displeasure (and that of the CFO), Rulebender quit before he could be fired. Martinet, whose knowledge of the consulting game was exceeded only by his ignorance of hospital computing, engaged a consultant in his own image. After finding out what Martinet wanted to hear, the consultant, who was being paid by the hour, took as long as he possibly could to tell him: Get rid of the network; give the financials the highest priority (the clinicals can wait); develop an organizational chart; institute a formidable number of regulations (for example, "Physicians Are Not Allowed in the Computing Room"); and of course keep him, the consultant, on retainer for the next six months, subject to renewal.

On the consultant's advice, Martinet hired an Assistant Vice President in Charge of Matrix Management, and replaced Rulebender with his old friend Mr. Binary, who was currently with Bison Computing, Inc. Upon Binary's arrival the network was disassembled and the hospital signed a multimillion-dollar contract with Bison for new computers. (There was a rumor that the consultant was on retainer with Bison.) The few remaining Type 1 administrators disappeared from the financial office and computing center and the computing deteriorated noticeably. The clinicians were promised new and better things in the future—Rulebender "couldn't manage and was out of touch with new technology," they were advised.

Binary moved quickly to form his organizational chart based on reorganization. He hired ten directors, each of whom hired two assistant directors, each of whom hired two managers. Now seventy of the rectangular boxes on his chart had names to go with them (eighty to go, once all the assistant managers were hired). "It takes a lot of people to downsize," he was heard to say.

What downsizing did occur was from the ranks of those who were doing the computing. Once reorganization was in progress and management had grown to respectable size, there were very few programmers or engineers for them to manage—about one worker for every ten managers. The competent programmers and engineers, who didn't want to report to people who knew nothing about computing, were following Rulebender out the door to jobs where competence was still in demand.

Something Must Be Done

After a while, with nothing to replace the computing they had lost, a few impatient doctors began to badger Mr. Binary for help. They couldn't locate the results of their laboratory tests—nothing happened when they turned on the high-resolution, multifaceted graphics terminals—and the new electronic mail system was inoperative. This put Mr. Binary in a bit of a bind. For one thing, he was not well versed in the subject of clinical computing. For another, his new computers were not well suited to clinical applications; they were better suited to matrix accounting. Mr. Binary knew he couldn't deliver.

To admit this inability, however, was to risk loss of control, perhaps even a clinical takeover. But he couldn't just say no. So he formed a committee, standing. He made himself chair and appointed a token doctor and a token nurse as two of the members. At the first meeting, he handed out the new organizational chart—five pages of rectangular boxes with interconnecting lines. He then announced with pride that he had gotten rid of the legacy systems (read "Rulebender's systems") and had signed a contract for more computers and additional consultation. Then he spoke for thirty-five minutes about the conversion of the hospital's financial programs to the new matrix billing system, replete with packages, client servers, open architecture, and connectivity—"In other words," he declared with pride, "we have a best-of-breed data warehouse." The token doctor and token nurse didn't know what this meant, but they didn't ask. They didn't want to prolong the meeting.

At the next meeting, Mr. Binary transferred the onus for clinical computing to the doctor and nurse with a writing assignment: "Document your needs in a memo," and asked each of them to serve as members on one of two newly formed subcommittees, "assistant director in charge of clinical services, chair." Binary followed up the meeting with a memo of his own, "dictated but not signed," stressing the importance of detailed documentation prepared in advance. In the meantime, if he got the bills out more or less on time, the CFO was pleased. Mr. Binary was off the hook.

Clinical Refugees

With time, however, the token doctor got impatient, as did the token nurse, the token pharmacist, and the token technologist. They had documented and redocumented their requests, but still they had no computing. They threatened to resign from the standing committee as well as the subcommittee. Mr. Binary had to make another move. This time he turned to the marketplace. If he could buy and install a "clinical package," he could retain control and ward off the critics. "Why reinvent the wheel?" he asked, stretching his capacity for metaphor.

A number of computer suppliers were more than willing to comply. One marketed what it called a total hospital information system (HIS). A look beyond the glossy brochure would have revealed a partial system that contained little information. But Mr. Binary didn't look. The acronyms were sufficient for his purpose, and he bought HIS and MIS. What he got, of course, was yet more hardware, a bigger budget, and a cumbersome billing system. What little clinical computing there was in HIS and MIS (one doctor mistakenly thought the M stood for medical) either didn't work or didn't fit the needs of the clinicians and patients.

But no matter, Martinet and the CFO were pleased, as was the CEO, when informed by memo, "dictated *and* signed"; they had something to announce. They scheduled a wine-and-cheese reception to honor HIS and MIS; they invited all the administrators, the regional vice president for sales at Bison Computing, Mr. Binary, who had been promoted to vice president and CIO, and as an afterthought, the token doctor and token nurse. Later, to save money, the hospital did some more downsizing, cutting back on nurses, pharmacists, laboratory technologists, and phlebotomists, and transferred their responsibilities to the remaining nurses and the interns and residents, who were too tired to protest. Mr. Binary, in turn, got the updated versions of HIS and MIS (HIS-U and MIS-U), hired ten more assistant managers, and had his office refurbished in cherry wood. Priorities were once again in administrative order.

But the doctors and patients were *not* pleased. Medical care was suffering. The doctors and nurses took their patients elsewhere. The financial picture deteriorated. No loans could be secured. No Type 1 employees could be found. At the point of terminus, there was one patient, suspended in a semianimated coma à la Robin Cook, surrounded by a thousand administrators. Shortly thereafter, Metropolitan closed its doors.

The CFO, Martinet, Binary, and the consultant had already left town. The three of them are working for Bison Computing, Inc. Rulebender has formed his own company (very lean on administrators), and has installed good computing in several hospitals.

—∿∿—

What then does the future hold for us? Are we destined to follow Martinet and Binary down the garden path? Or can we join forces with Rulebender?

CHAPTER ELEVEN

What Can Be Done

It used to be that one of the rewards of being a doctor was being your own boss. Today, however, many doctors work for other people. As a political force within hospitals and clinics, doctors and other clinicians are poorly organized. The few who do demand good computing are likely to find themselves on a sub (or sub-sub) committee, token members dutifully accepting their writing assignments. "Write me a memo" is the administrative mechanism by which nothing gets done.

For their part, patients commonly believe that the computer is in fact being used to its full capacity in hospitals and clinics. This misconception is promulgated by those members of the computing industry who advertise total hospital and management information systems, which are neither total nor clinically informative. It is also promulgated by Type 2 consultants, for whom prophecy is a substitute for accomplishment, and who will promise almost anything as long as a lucrative consulting contract is in the offing.

TAKING ACTION

It may be fair to accuse doctors and patients of failing to be assertive about clinical computing, but it is not fair to accuse them of computer phobia, computer illiteracy, or being too old to use modern technology. A computer program that clinicians or patients prefer not to use probably offers no advantage over traditional methods of processing and presenting information. Young or old, accustomed to the keyboard or not, clinicians (and patients) will turn readily to a computer that is helpful.

What the Clinician Can Do

But we clinicians must be more assertive. We must seek out the Type 1 administrators at our hospitals and clinics and convince them that good clinical computing is in their own best interest—that it will increase efficiency and save money as well as improving patient care.

Those of us who do research on computer applications in medicine have a special responsibility in this regard: to see that the benefits that are possible and those that have already been achieved are brought to the attention of clinicians and administrators alike. In hospitals where computers are used primarily for fiscal purposes, what computer to buy and what software to use are viewed as financial decisions. When a CFO or CIO—officials rarely familiar with the practice of medicine—selects the hospital's computing system, the needs of clinicians and patients are typically not considered in the decision. Once the benefits of good clinical computing are widely recognized, however, clinicians can insist on participating meaningfully in the selection of systems for their hospitals.

When the computing industry learns that hospitals will accept nothing but the best possible clinical computing, programs that truly help in the practice of medicine will become available in the marketplace.

Questions to Ask

When the decisions about computing are being shared and clinicians and administrators are working together to buy a system, they should first interview representatives of the prospective company. They should do this themselves, avoiding consultants and their biases. As a team, they must be willing to assume responsibility for the outcome of their decision, good or bad, and not pass this on to each other or to their colleagues.

As things stand now, it is difficult to glean from computer manufacturers and software suppliers the extent to which customers actually use their computing systems. Yet keeping track of use is something that a computer can easily be programmed to do. Is there something these companies have to hide? Do their accomplishments not live up to their promises?

One strategy is to ask the company representative where the system is working best. (I've noticed that the site of referral tends to be geographically remote from the point at which the question is asked; if you are in southern Florida, you can expect the site to be north of British Columbia.) Then call the hospital or clinic to verify that the system is in place. Then, if you possibly can, visit the hospital (be prepared for a long journey) and interview the users whom the system is designed to serve. It is important to speak with a user rather than the person who made the decision to buy, who is probably not a user and may be more interested in defending the purchase than in assessing its quality.

The questions to ask are straightforward: Does the system record usage, and if not, why not? How often is the computing being used, and by whom? How well is the computing liked? What is the effect of the computer on the hospital's finances? And what is its effect on patient care? If responses engender optimism, I would proceed. If not, I would turn to another company.

What the Patient Can Do

The patient as well as the doctor should bring pressure to bear on the powers that be. Does your doctor have ready access by computer to the results of diagnostic studies, to advice and consultation, and to the medical literature? Does the computer serve to protect your privacy? If not, why not? It is your right to have good computing in your hospital and clinic.

If the computer is to be more fully used as a patient's assistant, in the home and other places of convenience, substantial resources must be devoted to the effort. There will be fewer administrative barriers, however, than in hospitals and clinics. If patients, as consumers, purchasers, taxpayers, and voters, demand good clinical computing on-line, I am optimistic that it will be forthcoming.

A DREAM FOR THE FUTURE

I have a modest dream for the future, my own indulgence in wishing as a substitute for doing. This is how I'd like medical care to be practiced when I become a patient.

—⁓—

Gradually with time, all medical services will move out of the hospital to places of convenience for the patient. The hospital as we know it today—ever larger, more corporate, and more bureaucratic—will disappear. It will be unnecessary to concern ourselves with Mr. Binary and his administrative hierarchy. The clinical haven of the future (I call it the *clinhaven*) will be a decentralized facility, small and conveniently located within or adjacent to a residential area—urban, suburban, or rural—within walking distance for many patients. Stays in the clinhaven will be appropriate for the illness, and complex diagnostic and therapeutic procedures will be possible on an outpatient basis.

The clinhaven will be staffed by skilled, humanistic clinicians, who also run the facility. Medical students will train in the clinhaven. Doctors will make house calls. Clinicians and patients will know each others' names and will work together as friends. Administrators will be available as needed. The atmosphere will be convivial. Waiting time will be short. Parking will be plentiful.

The clinhaven will be equipped with the latest in medical technology, including good clinical computing. In design it will be more like a small local hospital rather than a mega medical center, but it will have all the necessary resources to provide comprehensive medical care.

There will be local governance, and for the most part prepaid financing, with provisions for patients who cannot pay. The quality of care will determine the financing, not the reverse. Confidentiality will be protected; *no* clinical information will be released to third-party payers, *whoever* they may be, without the patient's consent.

Much of medical care will then move back to the home. Using interactive computing in their homes, patients themselves will manage common important medical problems. Even complex laboratory tests, once solely in the province of the large medical center or commercial laboratory, will be done by the patient, with easy-to-use equipment kept at home. Costs will go down, and time will be saved. But most important, the quality of medical care will be high.

Epilogue

Alexis de Tocqueville once observed that Americans would do almost anything to avoid walking. On the way to town, for example, an American would wait an hour for a ride rather than walk the same distance in half the time. What the great French sociologist observed with bemusement in the nineteenth century would have boggled his mind in the twentieth. Automatic transportation is everywhere. Escalators, elevators, and moving walkways pervade our buildings, malls, and airports. In summertime, we can be seen shivering in place on our moving walkways in airtight enclosures, while fossil fuel combats the sun's energy. Outdoors, the sidewalk is absent from modern urban planning.

Those who visited the World's Fair in 1939 may recall how summarily the General Motors exhibit dismissed pedestrian (that is, "unimaginative") transportation. I rode with my father in wonder through the streamlined city of tomorrow, housed in a domed edifice adjacent to the Tyron and Perisphere, in the heart of Flushing Meadow. No one in this miniature industrial utopia was walking. For me, walking was "out" from then on. Any alternative was better—be it wagon, tricycle, or Irish mail (a toy handcar popular in my child-hood). Later, my friends and I would hitchhike to and from high school. The only thing more embarrassing than to be seen walking was to be caught riding in a car with your father or (God forbid!) mother.

A TALE OF TWO HOMES

Now that we are in the computer age, there is even less reason for us to walk about outside. I no longer have to go to work to use my com-puter; I have one at home. Our kitchen is automated, our television is interactive, and we can shop and bank on the Internet. American Ex-press may soon shorten its admonition to "Don't leave home." My wife and I worry about how we'll manage if our machines break down.

When the Machine Stops

In "The Machine Stops," written in 1909, E. M. Forster takes the theme of don't leave home to its ultimate conclusion. He portrays a future society in which the people have descended to underground quar-ters—one person per hexagonal room—where their day-to-day needs and desires are met by an all-pervasive, all-accommodating automa-ton, the Machine. They venture forth from their rooms with de-creasing frequency; there is little reason for them to do so. They can communicate with each other automatically, using transmitter, re-ceivers, the "pneumatic post," and "blue plates" (handheld terminals in modern terms) on which the Machine projects images as well as text. Food is delivered, and waste disposed of, automatically, ad libi-tum. Medical services are delivered on demand. Music, art, literature, and science, by means of Web-like audiovisual presentations—inter-active as well as didactic—are available at the touch of a switch. And the air is always fresh.

Eventually, people have no need to leave their abodes except for the purpose of procreation. (Forster did not foresee the use of artificial in-semination.) But the act of sex, no longer an act of love, is but a singu-lar carnal responsibility to be performed with dispatch. Getting back to one's hexagonal sanctum as quickly as possible is of the highest priority.

And there is little reason to move about, even within one's room. An armchair and a reading desk are the only pieces of furniture. At the press of a button a hot bath rises from the floor. A bed appears on demand. (Somnolence is the only available diurnal cue, the difference between night and day having lost its meaning.) There is little reason even to move about in the chair; it takes minimal exertion to operate the buttons and switches.

As electromechanical activity replaces physical activity, flab replaces muscle. Physical powers fall into disrepute; they carry the risk of restlessness, curiosity, and (Machine forbid) rebellion. "Homelessness," banishment without respirator (the lung no longer tolerates terrestrial air) to the earth's surface and certain doom, is the penalty for independent behavior. Babies, housed in public nurseries, are sacrificed if they seem unacceptably robust at birth. There is no religion.

Whereas much of the human motor system is now vestigial, the sensory apparatus remains intact. But the reality of the world outside is perceived, from within each room, from an increasingly remote perspective. Early on, those who want to see the sights or hear the sounds of the earth's surface need only listen to a gramophone or watch a "cinematophore"—a program produced firsthand by those few who do venture, with portable respirator and "egression permit," to the surface. Eventually, however, egression is forbidden and there is no further possibility of firsthand observation. And with time the gramophones and cinematophores are transformed (Turnerized, some might say) into increasingly inexact replicas—reruns devoid of original content.

And so it is with independent thought: "Beware of firsthand ideas" is now the dictum of the day. Ideas are better acquired thirdhand than secondhand, better fourthhand than thirdhand, and so on, in a transitive relationship. Original ideas are no longer an issue; those harboring them have been banished to Homelessness.

Early on, the people responsible for the workings of the Machine understand it in its entirety. As time passes, however, division of labor prevails—"The better a man knew his own duties upon it, the less he understood the duties of his neighbor"—until there comes that crucial moment when no single person in all the world understands the Machine as a whole. This is the symbolically pivotal transition in Forster's story, for all the people in the world are now truly dependent on the Machine for life and (muscleless) limb. And with dependence comes subservience: the governing body (the Central Committee) has become a puppet; the governed are now governed by the Machine.

The time is now ripe for religion, and so it comes to pass. Although people still recognize intellectually that their ancestors created the

Machine, they now behave as if the Machine created *them*. The word "religion" is avoided in conversation (teleconverse, if you will, conducted remotely from room to room), but it is clear that the Machine is now the object of worship.

In each room, on the reading desk next to the armchair, there is one lone volume, a survivor "from the ages of litter," the *Book of the Machine*. Published by the Central Committee, this manual provides instructions for every possible use of the Machine. It is "richly bound"—new versions more so than old ones—and, increasingly, a source of spiritual comfort to those who hold it and kiss it. Technological scripture in hand, the people pray: "O Machine! O Machine!"

Diversity in worship is understood and tolerated. Some pray to the blue optic plates, others to the sound equipment, others to the Mending Apparatus, with each person imploring one or another sacred device to intercede on his or her behalf with the Machine. But there is a minimum set of tenets required of all, regardless of sect: the "Undenominational Mechanism." And there is persecution. Heretics are threatened with Homelessness.

Vashti and her son Kuno are the central figures of the story. Vashti represents the rule. A conformist, comfortable with secondhand ideas, no longer capable of creative thought (and threatened and angered by those who still are), and devoid of muscle, she is philosophically at one with the Machine. Kuno, by contrast, is the exception—a renegade, independent in thought, creative in ideas, and physically active, he is philosophically wary of the Machine and continually at risk of Homelessness. As the story unfolds, Kuno calls his mother to his room (her one venture forth, done so with great reluctance) to tell her, much to her dismay, that he has climbed to the surface, up old ventilation shafts, without an egression permit and at great risk to life and limb. There he has seen life in the open air and under the sun.

For Kuno, the foray was worth the personal danger; for a brief moment in his life he was an individual, independent of the Machine. For Vashti, who wants to be spared the details of the odyssey, there is embarrassment for having mothered an ungrateful reprobate; she reproaches him angrily for breaking the rules. Kuno in turn reproves her for her unquestioning allegiance to the Machine. It goes on, back and forth. Still, during their quarrel the reader is aware of a bond, even a love, between them.

Finally, they return to their respective rooms, to visit each other no more. For the mother, life progresses peacefully; for the rebel son (we must surmise), there is increasing discontent.

Then one day, as the title of Forster's story so ominously portends, things begin to go awry. The problems are small at first but insidious—an irritating noise in a symphony from "the Brisbane school," a jarring sound emanating from an optic plate, a bit of mold on a piece of synthetic fruit (annoyances to which the people grudgingly adjust). The situation gets worse and worse, however, and with time the "stoppage" comes to interfere even with the necessities of life—a bed doesn't appear when summoned, a plate of food is inedible, and the air is no longer fresh.

People complain, but to no avail. The complaints are dutifully forwarded to the "Committee of the Mending Apparatus" (no mention of subcommittees, but we know they were there) and from there to the Central Committee, which responds with words of reassurance and a call for patience. But the situation continues to deteriorate, and at an augmented pace. The air is bad now and the lights are too dim for reading; people clutch the Book in their arms and pray in the darkness.

One day there is silence. The continuous, ubiquitous sound of the Machine—stimulus to every organ of Corti from the time of its inception—is gone, and the silence is terrifying. In panic, people vacate their rooms. But they cannot go far; the air is foul and the underground corridors are impassable—unlit and blocked with people struggling to move, trampling or being trampled, gasping for air or holding their breath, and dying. The Machine has stopped, and within minutes, humanity as it exists underground is extinct.

In their last few moments of life, Vashti and Kuno are reunited, and Forster offers his readers a glimmer of hope. Kuno tells his mother that when he ventured forth he saw people on the surface of the earth, living and breathing. And as the walls and ceilings collapse about them, Vashti and Kuno catch a glimpse of "untainted sky."

—⁓—

Even when Forster wrote this story in 1909, there were legitimate concerns about excessive reliance on technology in many aspects of people's lives. Still, it was the people's excessive reliance on the Machine, not the Machine itself, that led to the downfall of Forster's subterranean civilization. It can be argued that the Machine was capable of doing good, if employed with wisdom and restraint. For all the problems and ultimate horrors wrought by misuse of the Machine, Forster does say that medical services were delivered on demand. Such automated house calls, if used widely and coupled with healthy activity, would be welcome in modern times.

Let me turn now to an example of the positive influence of computer-assisted health care in the home.

When the Home Is Also the Clinic: The Tale of One Real Child

Whether medical care is primarily the responsibility of the doctor or the patient is often dictated by supply and demand. If the biochemistry of insulin or the physiology of the pancreas were such that a child with diabetes needed only one injection of insulin per year, it is likely that the diabetes expert in the academic medical center would administer the insulin, at the hospital and at considerable expense. If the child needed an injection every six months, the pediatrician would do it in the office; if every three months, the nurse practitioner. But the need is typically twice a day, and it is the parent or older child who gives the injection at home, with skill and without professional assistance. There is no other way.

On the other hand, the family needs guidance. When their clinical interactions occur in a doctor's office rather than their home, the doctor rarely sees their living situation. But this is where they will try to carry out the plans they have made in dialogue with the doctor. In other words, there may be a disparity between plans made in the controlled environment of a physician's examining room and the realities of life in the patient's home. My family and I have experienced this problem firsthand, and the interactive computer has been of great help to us at home.

Last January, our daughter and her husband noticed that their seventeen-month-old toddler, our grandson Sean, had been drinking a lot of water for several days and urinating heavily since the evening before; his diaper was soaked in the morning. Sean was alert and active, but Alison and Chris were concerned, observing parents as they are. They took Sean to the pediatrician. A urine test was positive for glucose. When they telephoned my wife and me, Alison and Chris were taking Sean (and their three-year-old, James) to the university hospital in the city for definitive diagnosis.

During Sean's brief stay in the hospital he was given excellent medical care. Insulin was administered, and Sean's blood glucose level and fluid and electrolyte imbalance were brought quickly under control. The doctors and nurses did their best to be pleasant. But there were problems with communication. Alison and Chris were given the instant short course on juvenile diabetes: doctors, doctors in training, nurses, nurses in training, nutritionists, nutritionists in training, and various auxiliary health care workers traipsed in and out of the little boy's room, each offering interpretations and advice from a new perspective. The upshot was a conflicting array of directives and advice: "Sean doesn't have to eat everything on the tray." "It's imperative that Sean eat everything on the tray." "You can always get in touch with the doctor when you need help." "We mustn't bother the doctor now." "Give him his insulin and wait a half hour before you feed him." "You don't have to wait before feeding him."

The importance of diet was emphasized, and in this case everyone agreed. Sean was to receive three meals a day, each containing forty-two grams of carbohydrate in roughly equal amounts of starch, dairy food, and fruit, with three snacks between meals (seven grams of carbohydrate in the morning, seven grams in the afternoon, and fifteen grams before bedtime). For Sean's first breakfast in the hospital, Alison and Chris dutifully ordered three-fourths of a cup of Cheerios (fifteen grams of carbohydrate), one cup of whole milk (twelve grams), and half a cup of orange juice (fifteen grams). A tray appeared with a bowl of grits, a glass of skim milk, two sausages, and a cup of black coffee.

I don't mean to imply that there was no effort at good communication. The interns and residents were helpful and sympathetic. The nurses were readily available day and night, doing their best to accommodate the patients and their families (there were many seriously ill children and concerned parents on the pediatric service). The nurses' instructions on using the glucometer and administering insulin were given with skill and patience. Alison and Chris learned quickly how to prick a finger, put a drop of blood on the strip, read the blood glucose determination, measure the insulin in a syringe, and give Sean the injection. A great many pamphlets and booklets appeared, some making sense and some not. Most of the reading material had been developed for older children; seventeen months is very young for the onset of diabetes.

Sean was discharged on the dietary program begun in the hospital (without the coffee) and a "sliding scale" formula for insulin. The senior physicians had made it clear that the goal was to keep his blood glucose between 100 and 200, difficult as this would be. They had not made it clear that this was an ideal goal; that meeting it consistently would be *impossible*. In addition, they had not explained that tight control of glucose levels would be much more important after puberty than before.

In young children with diabetes, if either end of the glucose spectrum, particularly the low end, can be avoided, this is good management. If the blood level can be kept between 100 and 200 *half the time*, that is about the best one can hope for. And even with the best-laid plans and under the best of circumstances, there will be wide, anxiety-provoking fluctuations between hyperglycemia and hypoglycemia. Parents must learn to live with this.

The first month at home was the hardest. But somehow the family got through it, with the help of relatives and friends. (Soon there was a new baby, Catherine.) The senior doctor's offer—"You can call us any time"—proved accurate; Alison and Chris *could* call them any time. But most of the time they were told to wait for a return phone call, and sometimes it never came.

On the first Saturday at home Sean was vomiting and took little by mouth. The doctor on call recommended altering the insulin dosage, giving Sean whatever he would take by mouth, and most important, giving him fluids if he could hold them down, to prevent dehydration. Sean was better on Sunday, but Monday morning he started vomiting again. This time the senior pediatric diabetologist came to the phone (his secretary cajoled him upon Alison's insistence). He proceeded to *scold* Alison for doing what his colleague had recommended two days before. Later that day, Alison and Chris took Sean back to the hospital for rehydration. Fortunately, the resident who had been their favorite doctor during the earlier hospitalization was on hand. She offered advice and comfort, and stayed by the bedside to supervise the administration of the intravenous fluids. Sean was back home in a few hours, much improved.

THE GLUCOMETER. Sean's insulin schedule is determined by his glucometer readings. Every morning he gets 2 units of long-acting insulin. This is combined with 1 unit of regular insulin if his glucose is 70 to 100 mg per deciliter, 1.5 units if his glucose is 101 to 150, 2 units if it's 151 to 200, 2.5 units if 201 to 300, and 3 units if over 300. In the evening he gets 1 unit of long-acting insulin together with 0.5 unit of regular insulin if the glucose is 101 to 150, 1 unit if 151 to 200, 1.5 units if 201 to 300, and 2 units if over 300.

The glucometer is a wonderful machine, a specialized handheld computer made available for home use some fifteen years ago. It boggles my mind to think of the management of diabetes before the glucometer was developed, when families had to rely on the presence or absence of glucose in the urine. There was a lot of guessing. If the urine was free of glucose, this could be good (normoglycemia) or bad (hypoglycemia). Insulin dosages were determined by the urinary glucose level, and with toddlers like Sean, the renal threshold for glucose can be quite variable. The traditional intermittent visit to the clinic for a venipuncture was more symbolic than practical; a single, random glucose value was hardly indicative of day-to-day control.

With the glucometer, Sean's blood glucose can be measured many times a day, before his insulin injection, before each meal, and whenever there is cause for worry—when he has an upper respiratory tract infection, for example—although his parents don't want to prick those little fingers more often than they have to. (Sean is too young to tell them how he feels; they will be relieved when he can say "I feel shaky.") His first glucometer required a large drop of blood, which was not always easy to elicit from a diminutive digit. Alison or Chris would put a warm compress on one of Sean's fingers to make a usable drop more likely. But sometimes they would have to prick a second finger, sometimes a third or fourth. Another parent (rather than a doctor) told Alison about the Glucometer Elite, a new measuring device that works with a small droplet of blood. This computer has made life much easier for Sean and his parents, who never have to prick Sean's finger a second time. Alison has passed this information on to other parents in her Juvenile Diabetes Foundation chat group on the Internet. (There is active research now being done on a noninvasive glucometer, which will be a godsend for insulin-dependent diabetics.)

Approaching the "terrible twos," Sean is beginning to assert his independence, and "no" has a prominent place in his vocabulary. He is particularly apt to use this word at mealtimes, which have special importance in the life of a diabetic child. It is imperative for Sean to eat after his insulin injection. His breakfast and dinner are to be eaten, in theory, after thirty minutes. I am saying "in theory" advisedly. On the one hand, there is the ideal, harmonious relationship between toddler and parent, with the calm, smiling parent measuring a blood glucose level of precisely 151 mg per deciliter, administering 4 units of insulin, and after thirty minutes, feeding forty-two grams of carbohydrate. This was the picture dictated by the staff of the academic division of pediatric diabetology. On the other hand, there is the reality of a little boy in his high chair in the dining room, lips tight, masseters fully contracted (mouth opening only for as long as it takes to say no to an approaching spoon)—the anxious interplay between an uncomprehending two-year old and a parent faced with the prospect of insulin shock.

THE PROBLEM. It's 7:30 in the morning. You and your little boy have the daily diabetes ordeal ahead of you. You place the equipment within easy reach and sit in a straight-backed chair. You call your child, who runs over and gives your leg a hug. You put him in your lap. You look at your notebook to check which finger to use. You swab the finger with alcohol, press the pricking device against it, distract your child with some gentle words, and press the button. He barely flinches; the spring action is well designed and the small lancet is very sharp. You touch his finger to the glucometer strip. He reaches for the pricking device. You quickly remove the lancet and let him grab the device, which he examines eagerly. Now *he's* in control. After thirty seconds, he says "beep." After forty-five seconds, the glucometer says "beep." You look at the reading anxiously—220. You relax.

Your boy hops down and runs about happily. You draw the insulin into the small syringe—2 units longacting, 2.5 units regular. This is tricky; the amounts are small and exact measurement is impossible. You just want to be as close as possible. You check your notebook again—"right thigh." You call the little guy again. He comes, but a little more slowly this time. He's up on your lap; you swab a place on his thigh, gently create a fold of skin, talk diversion-type talk, and inject the insulin. He whimpers briefly. You give him a hug. He gives you a hug. Breakfast in thirty minutes.

Your boy is now in his high chair. On the tray is a small bowl of Cheerios (fifteen grams of carbohydrate), carefully measured. "It's time for breakfast," you say with a smile, "You like Cheerios, don't you?" You look away for a moment and hear a forceful "No!" from the high chair. You turn back. The cereal is on the floor. You begin to worry;

the insulin is working and he needs to eat. You hand him his "Barney" cup—orange juice (fifteen grams), carefully measured. You turn to your other children for a moment. Bang, splash. You turn back. There's a big grin on Sean's face; he has tested the law of gravity and it holds. You move quickly to the kitchen, peel a banana—five inches (fifteen grams)—and hand it to him. He does his Roger Clemens windup. You retrieve the banana in the nick of time. You give him a small piece of it, which he eats. You relax a little. His appetite has prevailed. He eats his new serving of Cheerios, carefully measured. You relax a bit more. He drinks his milk. You are feeling better.

Two hours pass. It's time for his snack. He drinks his milk, a quarter of a cup (three grams), carefully measured. You give him a peanut cracker (four grams). He scurries off. Minutes later he returns empty-handed. Oh God! Did he eat it or drop it behind the couch? Should you check his blood glucose again? You decide to give him another cracker (too much is better than too little). He eats the cracker under your watchful eye and is off to play. In two hours it will be time for lunch.

A SOLUTION. The computer can be programmed to simulate the time-honored one-on-one conversation between patient and doctor. It can do this with the collective wisdom of many doctors and in a convenient place for the patient. In addition, with the thriving technology of worldwide communication, patients and parents of patients can use a keyboard to talk with doctors and other patients or parents, using their personal computers and the Internet at home. Alison and Chris are now regular users of news groups, mailing lists, and chat groups on the Internet. The new technology has given them companionship and reassurance as well as practical help with Sean. Despite the difficulties I have described, Sean and his family are doing very well. He is a beautiful, loving, brilliant little boy, if you will permit a grandfather's assessment.

CONCLUSION

I look forward to the time when doctors will leave their cloistered clinical environments, literally as well as by computer-based telecommunication, to familiarize themselves with the home environments of their patients, and thereby close the gap between prescription and implementation. For the pediatric diabetologist, an even more informative experience would be to raise a diabetic child. But short of this, first-hand knowledge of the day-to-day life of the patient and the patient's family could go a long way.

I am in complete agreement with Forster's admonition—all the more remarkable in that it was written in 1909—that abdication to a machine would lead to disaster. But Forster was not opposed to machines themselves; he appreciated the societal benefits of technology. He was opposed, as I am, to the loss of human control over machines. And we must guard against this with computers in medicine.

Whereas it is not necessary for users to understand the inner workings of computers, it is of the utmost importance for developers to understand the systems they develop, to recognize that they are responsible for their systems and accountable to their users, and make sure their bond of trust with their users is never broken.

For the user, the off button should always be placed in a prominent location. And of course we should all get plenty of fresh air and exercise.

⟶ Bibliography and Further Reading

Preface

Collen, M. F. *A History of Medical Informatics in the United States, 1950 to 1990*. Bethesda, Md.: American Medical Informatics Association, 1995.

Rogers, C. R. *Client-Centered Therapy*. Boston: Houghton Mifflin, 1965.

Shaw, G. B. *Man and Superman: A Comedy and a Philosophy*. Baltimore: Penguin, 1952.

Slack, W. V. "Patient Power." In J. A. Jacquez (ed.), *Computer Diagnosis and Diagnostic Methods: The Proceedings of the Second Conference on the Diagnostic Process Held at the University of Michigan*. Springfield, Ill.: Thomas, 1972.

Slack, W. V. "The Patient's Right to Decide." *Lancet*, 1977, *2*, 240.

Chapter One

Alcoholics Anonymous. New York: Alcoholics Anonymous Publishing, 1955.

Haggard, H. W. *Devils, Drugs, and Doctors*. Boston: Charles River Books, 1980.

Machiavelli, N. *The Prince*. (G. Bull, trans.). Harmondsworth, England: Penguin Books, 1981.

Slack, W. V. "Patient Counseling by Computer." In S. Zoog and S. Yarnall (eds.), *The Changing Health Care Team*. Seattle: Medical Communications and Services Association, 1976.

Slack, W. V. "Compugraphy." *M.D. Computing*, 1991, *8*(6), 342–346.

Slack, W. V. "When the Home Is Also the Clinic." *M.D. Computing*, 1996, *13*(6), 465–468.

Spock, B. *Dr. Spock's Baby and Child Care: Sixth Edition Fully Revised and Updated for the 1990s*. New York: NAL/Dutton, 1992.

Chapter Two

Angle, H. V., Johnson, T., Grebenkemper, N. S., and Ellinwood, E. H. "Computer Interview Support of Clinicians." *Professional Psychology,* Feb. 1979, pp. 49–57.

Baer, L., Brown-Beasley, M. W., Sorce, J., and Henriques, A. I. "Computer-Assisted Telephone Administration of a Structured Interview for Obsessive-Compulsive Disorder." *American Journal of Psychiatry,* 1993, *150*(11), 1737–1738.

Bana, D. S., Leviton, A., Swidler, C., Slack, W. V., and Graham, J. R. "A Computer-Based Headache Interview: Acceptance by Patients and Physicians." *Headache,* 1980, *20,* 85–89.

Bennett, S. E., Lawrence, R. S., Fleischmann, K. H., Gifford, C. S., and Slack, W. V. "Profile of Women Practicing Breast Self-Examination." *Journal of the American Medical Association,* 1983, *249*(4), 488–491.

Bleich, H. L. "The Kaiser Permanente Health Plan, Dr. Morris F. Collen, and Automated Multiphasic Testing." *M.D. Computing,* 1994, *11*(3), 136–139.

Bleich, H. L. "Wesley A. Clark, Charles E. Molnar, and the LINC." *M.D. Computing,* 1994, *11*(5), 269–270.

Brodman, K., Erdmann, A. J., Jr., Lorge, I., and Wolff, H. G. "Cornell Medical Index: Adjunct to Medical Interview." *Journal of the American Medical Association,* 1949, *140,* 530–534.

Brodman, K., Van Woerkom, A. J., Erdmann, A. J., Jr., and Goldstein, L. S. "Interpretation of Symptoms with a Data-Processing Machine." *Archives of Internal Medicine,* 1959, *103,* 776–782.

Carr, A. C., Ghosh, A., and Aneill, R. J. "Can a Computer Take a Psychiatric History?" *Psychological Medicine,* 1983, *13,* 151–158.

Chun, R.W.M., Van Cura, L. J., Spencer, M., and Slack, W. V. "Computer Interviewing of Patients with Epilepsy." *Epilepsy,* 1976, *17,* 371–375.

Clark, W. A., and Molnar, C. E. "A Description of the LINC." In R. W. Stacy and B. D. Waxman (eds.), *Computers in Biomedical Research.* Vol 2. New York: Academic Press, 1965.

Coddington, R. D., and King, T. L. "Automated History Taking in Child Psychiatry." *American Journal of Psychiatry,* 1972, *129,* 52–58.

Collen, M. F., Rubin, L., Neyman, J., Dantzig, G. B., Baer, R. M., and Siegelaub, A. B. "Automated Multiphasic Screening and Diagnosis." *American Journal of Public Health,* 1964, *54,* 741–750.

Coombs, G. J., Murray, W. R., and Krahn, D. W. "Automated Medical Histories: Factors Determining Patient Performance." *Computers and Biomedical Research,* 1970, *3,* 178–181.

Erdman, H. P., Klein, M. H., and Greist, J. H. "Direct Patient Computer Interviewing." *Journal of Consulting and Clinical Psychology,* 1985, *53,* 760–773.

Evans, S., and Gormican, A. "The Computer in Retrieving Dietary History Data." *Journal of the American Dietetic Association,* 1973, *63,* 397–407.

Gottlieb, G. L., Beers, R. F., Bernecker, C., and Samter, M. "An Approach to Automation of Medical Interviews." *Computers and Biomedical Research,* 1972, *5,* 99–107.

Greist, J. H., Gustafson, D. H., Erdman, H. P., Taves, J. E., Klein, M. H., and Speidel, S. D. "Suicide Risk Prediction by Computer Interview: A Prospective Study." *American Journal of Psychiatry,* 1973, *130,* 1327–1332.

Greist, J. H., and Klein, M. H. "Computer Programs for Patients, Clinicians, and Researchers in Psychiatry." In J. B. Sidowski, J. H. Johnson, and T. A. Williams (eds.), *Technology in Mental Health Care Delivery Systems.* Norwood, Conn.: Ablex, 1980.

Greist, J. H., Klein, M. H., and Van Cura, L. J. "A Computer Interview for Psychiatric Patient Target Symptoms." *Archives of General Psychiatry,* 1973, *29,* 247–253.

Grossman, J. H., Barnett, G. O., McGuire, M. T., and Swedlow, D. B. "Evaluation of Computer-Acquired Patient Histories." *Journal of the American Medical Association,* 1971, *215*(8), 1286–1291.

Hasley, S. "A Comparison of Computer-Based Personal Interviews for the Gynecologic History Update." *Obstetrics and Gynecology,* 1995, *84*(4), 494–498.

Haug, P. J., Warner, H. R., Clayton, P. D., Schmidt, C. D., Pearl, J. E., Farney, R. J., Crapo, R. O., Tocino, I., Morrison, W. J., and Frederick, P. R. "A Decision-Driven System to Collect the Patient History." *Computers and Biomedical Research,* 1987, *20,* 193–207.

Hicks, G. P., Gieschen, M. M., Slack, W. V., and Larson, F. C. "Routine Use of a Small Digital Computer in the Clinical Laboratory." *Journal of the American Medical Association,* 1966, *196,* 973–978.

Houziaux, M. O., and Lefebve, P. J. "Historical and Methodological Aspects of Computer-Assisted Medical History Taking." *Medical Informatics (London),* 1986, *11,* 129–143.

Jacquez, J. A. (ed.). *Computer Diagnosis and Diagnostic Methods: The Proceedings of the Second Conference on the Diagnostic Process Held at the University of Michigan.* Springfield, Ill.: Thomas, 1972.

Linberg, G., Seensalu, R., Nilsson, L. H., Forsell, P., Kagar, L., and Knill-Jones, R. P. "Transferability of a Computer System for Medical

History Taking and Decision Support in Dyspepsia: A Comparison of Indicants for Peptic Ulcer Disease." *Scandinavian Journal of Gastroenterology Supplement,* 1987, *128,* 190–196.

Lucas, R. W., Mullin, P. J., Luna, C.B.X., and McInroy, D. C. "Psychiatrists and a Computer as Interrogators of Patients with Alcohol-Related Illnesses: A Comparison." *British Journal of Psychiatry,* 1977, *131,* 160–167.

Lutner, R. E., Roizen, M. F., Stocking, C. B., Thisted, R. A., Kim, S., Duke, P. C., Pompei, P., and Kassel, C. K. "The Automated Interview Versus the Personal Interview: Do Patient Responses to Preoperative Health Questions Differ?" *Anesthesiology,* 1991, *75*(3), 394–400.

Maultsby, M. C., and Slack, W. V. "A Computer-Based Psychiatry History System." *Archives of General Psychiatry,* 1971, *25,* 570–572.

Mayne, J. G., Weksel, W., and Sholtz, P. N. "Toward Automating the Medical History." *Mayo Clinic Proceedings,* 1968, *43,* 1–25.

Millstein, S. G., and Irwin, C. E., Jr. "Acceptability of Computer-Acquired Sexual Histories in Adolescent Girls." *Journal of Pediatrics,* 1983, *103,* 815–819.

Pauker, S. G., Gorry, G. A., Kassirer, J. P., and Schwartz, W. B. "Towards the Simulation of Clinical Cognition: Taking a Present Illness by Computer." *American Journal of Medicine,* 1976, *60,* 981–996.

Peckham, B. M., Slack, W. V., Carr, W. F., Van Cura, L. J., and Schultz, A. E. "Computerized Data Collection in the Management of Uterine Cancer." *Clinical Obstetrics and Gynecology,* 1967, *10,* 1003–1015.

Pringle, M. "Using Computers to Take Patient Histories." *British Medical Journal,* 1988, *297,* 697–698.

Quaak, M. J., Westerman, R. F., Schout, J. A., Hasman, A., and van Bemmel, J. H. "Patient Appreciations of Computerized Medical Interviews." *Medical Informatics (London),* 1986, *11,* 339–350.

Savage, L. J. "Diagnosis and the Bayesian Viewpoint." In J. A. Jacquez (ed.), *Computer Diagnosis and Diagnostic Methods: The Proceedings of the Second Conference on the Diagnostic Process Held at the University of Michigan.* Springfield, Ill.: Thomas, 1972.

Skinner, H. A., and Allen, B. A. "Does the Computer Make a Difference? Computerized Versus Face-to-Face Versus Self-Report Assessment of Alcohol, Drug, and Tobacco Use." *Journal of Consulting and Clinical Psychology,* 1983, *51*(2), 267–275.

Slack, W. V. "Patient Power." In J. A. Jacquez (ed.), *Computer Diagnosis and Diagnostic Methods: The Proceedings of the Second Conference on the*

Diagnostic Process Held at the University of Michigan. Springfield, Ill.: Thomas, 1972.

Slack, W. V. "The Patient's Right to Decide." *Lancet,* 1977, *2,* 240.

Slack, W. V. "A History of Computerized Medical Interviews." *M.D. Computing,* 1984, *1*(5), 52–59, 68.

Slack, W. V. "Measurement of Intelligence: Misplaced Trust and the Lure of Prophecy." *M.D. Computing,* 1995, *12*(5), 363–372.

Slack, W. V. "Brave New Interviewer." *Harvard Medical Alumni Bulletin,* 1996, *69*(4), 44–49.

Slack, W. V., Hicks, G. P., Reed, C. E., and Van Cura, L. J. "A Computer-Based Medical History System." *New England Journal of Medicine,* 1966, *274*(4), 194–198.

Slack, W. V., Leviton, A., Bennett, S. E., Fleischmann, K. H., and Lawrence, R. S. "Relation Between Age, Education, and Time to Respond to Questions in a Computer-Based Medical Interview." *Computers and Biomedical Research,* 1988, *21,* 78–84.

Slack, W. V., and Van Cura, L. J. "Computer-Based Patient Interviewing. Parts I & II." *Postgraduate Medicine,* 1968, *43,* 68–74, 115–120.

Slack, W. V., and Van Cura, L. J. "Patient Reaction to Computer-Based Medical Interviewing." *Computers and Biomedical Research,* 1968, *1,* 527–531.

Stead, W. W., Hammond, W. E., and Estes, E. H. "Evaluation of an Audio Mode of the Automated Medical History." *Methods of Information in Medicine,* 1977, *16,* 20–23.

Stead, W. W., Heyman, A., Thompson, H. K., and Hammond, W. E. "Computer-Assisted Interview of Patients with Functional Headaches." *Archives of Internal Medicine,* 1972, *129,* 1–12.

Van Cura, L. J., Jensen, N. M., Greist, J. H., Lewis, W. R., and Frey, S. R. "Venereal Disease: Interviewing and Teaching by Computer." *American Journal of Public Health,* 1975, *65,* 1159–1164.

Wald, J. S., Rind, D., Safran, C., Kowaloff, H., Barker, R., and Slack, W. V. "Patient Entries in the Electronic Medical Record: An Interactive Interview Used in Primary Care." In R. M. Gardner (ed.), *American Medical Informatics Association: The Proceedings of the Nineteenth Annual Symposium on Computer Applications in Medical Care.* Philadelphia: Hanley & Belfus, 1995.

Warner, H. R., Rutherford, B. D., and Houtchens, B. A. "A Sequential Bayesian Approach to History Taking and Diagnosis." *Computers and Biomedical Research,* 1972, *5,* 256–262.

Chapter Three

Barry, M. J., Fowler, F. J., Jr., Mulley, A. G., Jr., Henderson, J. V., Jr., and Wennberg, J. E. "Patient Reaction to a Program Designed to Facilitate Patient Participation in Treatment Decisions for Benign Prostatic Hyperplasia." *Medical Care,* 1995, *33*(8), 771–782.

Bleich, H. L., Beckley, R. F., Horowitz, G., Jackson, J., Moody, E., Franklin, C., Goodman, S. R., McKay, M. W., Pope, R. A., Walden, T., Bloom, S. A., and Slack, W. V. "Clinical Computing in a Teaching Hospital." *New England Journal of Medicine,* 1985, *312*(12), 756–764.

Bloom, S., White, R., Beckley, R., and Slack, W. "Converse: A Means to Write, Edit, Administer and Summarize Computer-Based Dialogue." *Computers and Biomedical Research,* 1978, *11,* 167–175.

Brennan, P. F., Ripich, S., and Moore, S. M. "The Use of Home-Based Computers to Support Persons Living with AIDS/ARC." *Journal of Community Health Nursing,* 1991, *8*(1), 3–14.

Fisher, L. A., Johnson, T. S., Porter, D., Bleich, H. L., and Slack, W. V. "Collection of a Clean Voided Urine Specimen: A Comparison Among Spoken, Written, and Computer-Based Instructions." *American Journal of Public Health,* 1977, *67,* 640–644.

Gustafson, D. H., Bosworth, K., Hawkins, R. P., Boberg, E. W., and Bricker, E. "CHESS: A Computer-Based System for Providing Information, Referrals, Decision Support and Social Support to People Facing Medical and Other Health-Related Crises." In M. E. Frisse (ed.), *Proceedings of the Sixteenth Annual Symposium on Computer Applications in Medical Care.* Baltimore: American Medical Informatics Association, 1992.

Lieberman, J. A., III. "Compliance Issues in Primary Care." *Journal of Clinical Psychiatry Supplement,* 1996, *57*(7), 76–82.

Mulley, A. G. "Supporting the Patient's Role in Decision Making." *Journal of Occupational Medicine,* 1990, *32*(12), 1227–1228.

Slack, W. V. "Patient Counseling by Computer." In S. Zoog and S. Yarnall (eds.), *The Changing Health Care Team.* Seattle: Medical Communications and Services Association, 1976.

Slack, W. V. "The Patient's Right to Decide." *Lancet,* 1977, *2,* 240.

Slack, W., Porter, D., Witschi, J., Sullivan, M., Buxbaum, R., and Stare, F. "Dietary Interviewing by Computer: An Experimental Approach to Counseling." *Journal of the American Dietetic Association,* 1976, *69,* 514–517.

Slack, W. V., Safran, C., Kowaloff, H. B., Pearce, J., and Delbanco, T. L. "A Computer-Administered Health Screening Interview for Hospital Personnel." *M.D. Computing,* 1995, *12*(1), 25–30.

Stamm, W. E. "Urinary Tract Infections and Pyelonephritis." In K. J. Isselbacher and others (eds.), *Harrison's Principles of Internal Medicine.* (13th ed.) New York: McGraw-Hill, 1994.

Witschi, J. C., Kowaloff, H. B., and Slack, W. V. "An Interactive Dietary Interview for Hospital Employees." *M.D. Computing,* 1993, *104,* 216–224.

Witschi, J., Porter, D., Vogel, S., Buxbaum, R., Stare, F. J., and Slack, W. "A Computer-Based Dietary Counseling System." *Journal of the American Dietetic Association,* 1976, *69,* 385–390.

Chapter Four

Baer, L., Brown-Beasley, M. W., Sorce, J., and Henriques, A. I. "Computer-Assisted Telephone Administration of a Structured Interview for Obsessive-Compulsive Disorder." *American Journal of Psychiatry,* 1993, *150*(11), 1737–1738.

Beck, A. T., Rush, A. J., Shaw, B. F., and Emery, G. *Cognitive Therapy of Depression.* New York: Guilford Press, 1979.

Bergeron, B., and Locke, S. E. "Speech Recognition as a User Interface." *M.D. Computing,* 1990, *6*(1), 329–334.

Berne, E. *Transactional Analysis in Psychotherapy.* New York: Grove Press, 1961.

Blood, G. W. "A Behavioral-Cognitive Therapy Program for Adults Who Stutter: Computers and Counseling." *Journal of Communication Disorders,* 1995, *28*(2), 165–185.

Bloom, S., White, R., Beckley, R., and Slack, W. "Converse: A Means to Write, Edit, Administer and Summarize Computer-Based Dialogue." *Computers and Biomedical Research,* 1978, *11,* 167–175.

Campbell, D. T., and Stanley, J. C. *Experimental and Quasi-Experimental Designs for Research.* Chicago: Rand McNally, 1963.

Clark, W. A., and Molnar, C. E. "A Description of the LINC." In R. W. Stacy and B. D. Waxman (eds.), *Computers in Biomedical Research.* Vol 2. New York: Academic Press, 1965.

Colby, K. M., Watt, J. B., and Gilbert, J. P. "A Computer Method of Psychotherapy: Preliminary Communication." *Journal of Nervous and Mental Diseases,* 1966, *142,* 148–152.

Dinoff, M., Clark, C. G., Reitman, L. M., and Smith, R. E. "The Feasibility of Videotape Interviewing." *Psychological Reports,* 1969, *25,* 239–242.

Ellis, A. "The Essence of Rational Therapy." In B. N. Ard, Jr. (ed.), *Counseling and Psychotherapy: Classics on Theories and Issues.* Palo Alto, Calif.: Science and Behavior Books, 1966.

Erdman, H. P., Klein, M. H., and Greist, J. H. "Direct Patient Computer Interviewing." *Journal of Consulting and Clinical Psychology,* 1985, *53,* 760–773.

Freud, S. *A General Introduction to Psychoanalysis.* (J. Riviere, trans.). New York: Pocket Books, 1921.

Gendlin, E. T. *Experiencing and the Creation of Meaning.* New York: Free Press, 1962.

Glasser, W. "Reality Therapy: A Realistic Approach to the Young Offender." In B. N. Ard, Jr. (ed.), *Counseling and Psychotherapy: Classics on Theories and Issues.* Palo Alto, Calif.: Science and Behavior Books, 1966.

Gould, R. L. "The Use of Computers in Therapy." In T. Trabin and M. A. Freeman (eds.), *The Computerization of Behavioral Healthcare: How to Enhance Clinical Practice, Management, and Communications.* San Francisco: Jossey-Bass, 1996.

Hofmann, M., Hock, C., and Muller-Spahn, F. "Computer-Based Cognitive Training in Alzheimer's Disease Patients." *Annals of the New York Academy of Science,* 1996, *777,* 249–254.

Locke, S., Kowaloff, H. B., Hoff, R. G., Safran, C., Popovsky, M. A., Cotton, D. J., Finkelstein, D. M., Page, P. L., and Slack, W. V. "Computer-Based Interview for Screening Blood Donors for Risk of HIV Transmission." *Journal of the American Medical Association,* 1992, *268,* 1301–1305.

Lucas, R. W., Mullin, P. J., Luna, C.B.X., and McInroy, D. C. "Psychiatrists and a Computer as Interrogators of Patients with Alcohol-Related Illnesses: A Comparison." *British Journal of Psychiatry,* 1977, *131,* 160–167.

Maultsby, M. C. *Rational Behavior Therapy.* Englewood Cliffs, N.J.: Prentice Hall, 1984.

Maultsby, M. C., and Slack, W. V. "A Computer-Based Psychiatry History System." *Archives of General Psychiatry,* 1971, *25,* 570–572.

Millstein, S. G., and Irwin, C. E., Jr. "Acceptability of Computer-Acquired Sexual Histories in Adolescent Girls." *Journal of Pediatrics,* 1983, *103,* 815–819.

Mora, G. "History of Psychiatry." In H. I. Kaplan and B. J. Sadock (eds.), *Comprehensive Textbook of Psychiatry*. (4th ed.) Baltimore: Williams & Wilkins, 1985.

Pearson, J. S., Rome, H. P., Swenson, W. M., Mataya, P., and Brannick, T. L. "Development of a Computer System for Scoring and Interpretation of Minnesota Multiphasic Personality Inventories in a Medical Clinic." *Annals of the New York Academy of Science*, 1965, *126*(2), 684–695.

Rogers, C. R. *Client-Centered Therapy*. Boston: Houghton Mifflin, 1965.

Rosenthal, R. *Experimenter Effects in Behavioral Research*. Englewood Cliffs, N.J.: Appleton-Century-Crofts, 1966.

Rothbaum, B. O., Hodges, L. F., Kooper, R., Opdyke, D., Williford, J. S., and North, M. "Effectiveness of Computer-Generated (Virtual Reality) Graded Exposure in the Treatment of Acrophobia." *American Journal of Psychiatry*, 1995, *153*(4), 626–628.

Selmi, P. M., Klein, M. H., Greist, J. H., Sorrell, S. P., and Erdman, H. P. "Computer-Administered Cognitive-Behavioral Therapy for Depression." *American Journal of Psychiatry*, 1990, *147*(1), 51–56.

Sheridan, T. B., and Zeltzer, D. "Virtual Environments." *M.D. Computing*, 1994, *11*(5), 307–310.

Skinner, B. F. *Science and Human Behavior*. New York: Macmillan, 1953.

Slack, C. W. "Experimenter-Subject Psychotherapy: A New Method of Introducing Intensive Office Treatment for Unreachable Cases." *Mental Hygiene*, 1960, *44*, 238–256.

Slack, C. W., and Slack, W. V. "Good! We Are Listening to You Talk About Your Sadness." *Psychology Today*, 1974, *7*, 62–65.

Slack, W. V. "Patient Counseling by Computer." In S. Zoog and S. Yarnall (eds.), *The Changing Health Care Team*. Seattle: Medical Communications and Services Association, 1976.

Slack, W. V., Porter, D., Balkin, P., Kowaloff, H. B., and Slack, C. W. "Computer-Assisted Soliloquy as an Approach to Psychotherapy." *M.D. Computing*, 1990, *7*(1), 37–58.

Slack, W. V., and Slack, C. W. "Patient-Computer Dialogue." *New England Journal of Medicine*, 1972, *286*, 1304–1309.

Slack, W. V., and Slack, C. W. "Talking to a Computer About Emotional Problems: A Comparative Study." *Psychotherapy Theory Research and Practice*, 1977, *14*, 156–164.

Spielberger, C. D., Gorsuch, R. L., and Lushene, R. E. *STAI Manual for the State-Trait Anxiety Inventory ("Self-Evaluation Questionnaire.")* Palo Alto, Calif.: Consulting Psychologists Press, 1970.

Taylor, J. A. "A Personality Scale of Manifest Anxiety." *Journal of Abnormal Social Psychology,* 1953, *48,* 285–290.

Watson, J. B. *Behaviorism.* New York: Norton, 1924.

Webb, J. T. "Interview Synchrony: An Investigation of Two Speech Measures in an Automated Standardized Interview." In A. W. Siegman and R.A.B Pope (eds.), *Studies in Dyadic Communication.* New York: Pergamon Press, 1972.

Weizenbaum, J. *Computer Power and Human Reason.* New York: Freeman, 1976.

Chapter Five

Ferguson, T. *Health Online: How to Find Health Information, Support Groups, and Self-Help Communities in Cyberspace.* Reading, Mass.: Addison-Wesley, 1996.

Frisse, M. E., Kelly, E. A., and Metcalfe, E. S. "An Internet Primer: Resources and Responsibilities." *Academic Medicine,* 1994, *69,* 20–24.

Hahn, H., and Stout, R. *The Internet Complete Reference.* New York: McGraw-Hill, 1994.

Kehoe, B. P. *Zen and the Art of the Internet: A Beginner's Guide.* (3rd ed.) Englewood Cliffs, N.J.: Prentice Hall, 1994.

Krol, E. *The Whole Internet User's Guide and Catalog.* (2nd ed.) Sebastopol, Calif.: O'Reilly, 1994.

Levine, J. R., and Baroudi, C. *The Internet for Dummies.* San Mateo, Calif.: IDG Books Worldwide, 1993.

Maxwell, C., and Jan Grycz, C. *New Riders' Official Internet Yellow Pages.* Indianapolis, Ind.: New Riders, 1995.

"Medical Hardware and Software Buyers Guide." *M.D. Computing,* 1996, *13*(6), 486–576.

Pannen, M. "Guide to the Internet: The World Wide Web." *British Medical Journal,* 1995, *311,* 1552–1556.

Scolamiero, S. J. "Support Groups in Cyberspace." *M.D. Computing,* 1996, *14*(1), 12–17.

Slack, W. V. "The Handheld Calculator." *M.D. Computing,* 1991, *8,* 8–10.

Zelingher, J. "Exploring the Internet." *M.D. Computing,* 1995, *12*(2), 100–108.

Chapter Six

Aller, R. D., Robboy, S. J., Poitras, J. W., Altshuler, B. S., Cameron, M., Prior, M. C., Miao, S., and Barnett, G. O. "Computer-Assisted Pathology

Encoding and Reporting System (CAPER)." *American Journal of Clinical Pathology,* 1977, *68,* 715–720.

Anderson, J. G., and Jay, S. J. *Use and Impact of Computers in Clinical Medicine.* New York: Springer-Verlag, 1987.

Bakker, A. R. "The Development of an Integrated and Co-Operative Hospital Information System." *Medical Informatics (London),* 1984, *9,* 135–142.

Ball, M. J., Douglas, J. V., O'Desky, R. I., and Albright, J. W. *Healthcare Information Management Systems: A Practical Guide.* New York: Springer-Verlag, 1991.

Barnett, G. O. "The Application of Computer-Based Medical Record Systems in Ambulatory Practice." *New England Journal of Medicine,* 1984, *9,* 135–142.

Bleich, H. L. "The Kaiser Permanente Health Plan, Dr. Morris F. Collen, and Automated Multiphasic Testing." *M.D. Computing,* 1994, *11,* 136–139.

Bleich, H. L., Beckley, R. F., Horowitz, G., Jackson, J., Moody, E., Franklin, C., Goodman, S. R., McKay, M. W., Pope, R. A., Walden, T., Bloom, S. A., and Slack, W. V. "Clinical Computing in a Teaching Hospital." *New England Journal of Medicine,* 1985, *312*(12), 756–764.

Bleich, H. L., Safran, C., and Slack, W. V. "Departmental and Laboratory Computing in Two Hospitals." *M.D. Computing,* 1989, *6,* 149–155.

Bleich, H. L., and Slack, W. V. "Clinical Computing." *M.D. Computing,* 1989, *6,* 133–135.

Bleich, H. L., and Slack, W. V. "Designing a Hospital Information System: A Comparison of Interfaced and Integrated Systems." *M.D. Computing,* 1992, *9*(5), 293–296.

Clayton, P. D., Sideli, R. V., and Sengupta, S. "Open Architecture and Integrated Information at Columbia-Presbyterian Medical Center." *M.D. Computing,* 1992, *9*(5), 297–303.

Colby, K. M., Watt, J. B., and Gilbert, J. P. "A Computer Method of Psychotherapy: Preliminary Communication." *Journal of Nervous and Mental Diseases,* 1966, *142,* 148–152.

Collen, M. F. "The Multitest Laboratory in Health Care of the Future." *Hospitals,* 1967, *41,* 119–125.

Collen, M. F. *A History of Medical Informatics in the United States, 1950 to 1990.* Bethesda, Md.: American Medical Informatics Association, 1995.

Collen, M. F., Rubin, L., Neyman, J., Dantzig, G. B., Baer, R. M., and Siegelaub, A. B. "Automated Multiphasic Screening and Diagnosis." *American Journal of Public Health,* 1964, *54,* 741–750.

Feinstein, A. R. *Clinical Judgment.* Baltimore: Williams & Wilkins, 1967.

Gardner, R. M. "Collaboration in Clinical Computing at LDS Hospital." *M.D. Computing,* 1994, *11,* 10–13.

Glaser, J. P., Beckley, R. F., III, Roberts, P., Mara, J. K., Hiltz, F. L., and Hurley, J. "A Very Large PC LAN as the Basis for a Hospital Information System." *Journal of Medical Systems,* 1991, *15*(2), 133–137.

Gouveia, W. A., Diamantis, C., and Barnett, G. O. "Computer Applications in the Hospital Medication System." *American Journal of Hospital Pharmacy,* 1969, *26,* 140–150.

Greenes, R. A., Pappalardo, A. N., Marble, C. W., and Barnett, G. O. "Design and Implementation of a Clinical Data Management System." *Computers and Biomedical Research,* 1969, *2,* 469–485.

Greenes, R. A., and Shortliffe, E. H. "Medical Informatics: An Emerging Academic Discipline and Institutional Priority." *Journal of the American Medical Association,* 1990, 263, 1114–1120.

Grossman, J. H., Barnett, G. O., Koepsell, T. D., Nesson H. R., Dorsey, J. L., and Phillips, R. R. "An Automated Medical Record System." *Journal of the American Medical Association,* 1973, *224,* 1616–1621.

Hadley, T. P., Geer, D. E., Bleich, H. L., and Freedberg, I. M. "The Use of Digital Computers in Dermatological Diagnosis: Computer-Aided Diagnosis of Febrile Illness with Eruption." *Journal of Investigative Dermatology,* 1974, *62,* 467–472.

Hammond, W. E. "The Status of Healthcare Standards in the United States." *International Journal of Biomedical Computing,* 1995, *39,* 87–92.

Hendrickson, G., Anderson, R. K., Clayton, P. D., Cimino, J., Hripcsak, G. M., Johnson, S. B., McCormack, M., Sengupta, S., Shea, S., Sideli, R., and Roderer, N. "The Integrated Academic Information Management System at Columbia-Presbyterian Medical Center." *M.D. Computing,* 1992, *9,* 35–42.

Hicks, G. P., Gieschen, M. M., Slack, W. V., and Larson, F. C. "Routine Use of a Small Digital Computer in the Clinical Laboratory." *Journal of the American Medical Association,* 1966, *196,* 973–978.

Jacquez, J. A. (ed.). *The Diagnostic Process: Proceedings of Conference Held at the University of Michigan.* Ann Arbor: Malloy Lithographing, 1964.

Jacquez, J. A. (ed.). *Computer Diagnosis and Diagnostic Methods: The Proceedings of the Second Conference on the Diagnostic Process Held at the University of Michigan.* Springfield, Ill.: Thomas, 1972.

Karpinski, R. H., and Bleich, H. L. "MISAR: A Miniature Information Storage and Retrieval System." *Computers and Biomedical Research,* 1971, 4, 655–660.

Ledley, R. S., and Lusted, L. B. "Reasoning Foundations of Medical Diagnosis." *Science,* 1959, *130,* 9–21.

Leeming, B. W., Simon, M., Jackson, J. D., Horowitz, G. L., and Bleich, H. L. "Advances in Radiological Reporting Computerized Language Information Processing (CLIP)." *Radiology,* 1979, *133*(2), 349–353.

Lindberg, D. A. "Collection, Evaluation, and Transmission of Hospital Laboratory Data." *Methods of Information in Medicine,* 1967, *6,* 97–107.

Lindberg, D. A., and Humphreys, B. L. "Computers in Medicine." *Journal of the American Medical Association,* 1995, *273,* 1667–1668.

Lipkin, M., Engle, R. L., Jr., Flehinger, B. J., Gerstman, L. J., and Atamer, M. A. "Computer-Aided Differential Diagnosis of Hematologica Diseases." *Annals of the New York Academy of Science,* 1969, *161,* 670–679.

Lodwick, G. S., Turner, A. H., Lusted, L. B., and Templeton, A. W. "Computer-Aided Analysis of Radiographic Images." *Journal of Chronic Disease,* 1966, *19,* 485–496.

Lusted, L. B. *Introduction to Medical Decision Making.* Springfield, Ill.: Thomas, 1968.

McDonald, C. J., Murray, R., Jeris, D., Bhargave, B., Seeger, J., and Blevins, L. "A Computer-Based Record and Clinical Monitoring System for Ambulatory Care." *American Journal of Public Health,* 1977, *67,* 240–245.

McDonald, C. J., Tierney, W. M., Overhage, J. M., Martin, D. K., and Wilson, G. "The Regenstrief Medical Record System: 20 Years of Experience in Hospitals, Clinics, and Neighborhood Health Centers." *M.D. Computing,* 1992, *9,* 206–218.

Melski, J. W., Geer, D. E., and Bleich, H. L. "Medical Information Storage and Retrieval Using Preprocessed Variables." *Computers and Biomedical Research,* 1978, *11,* 613–621.

Orthner, H. F., and Blum, B. I. *Implementing Health Care Information Systems.* New York: Springer-Verlag, 1989.

Pauker, S. G., And Kassirer, J. P. "Therapeutic Decision Making: A Cost-Benefit Analysis. *New England Journal of Medicine,* 1975, *293,* 229–234.

Pope, R. A., Mattson, C. J., Janousek, J., and Slack, W. V. "A Computer-Based IV Admixture System." *Methods of Information in Medicine,* 1982, *21*(2), 65–69.

Pryor, T. A., Gardner, R. M., Clayton, P. D., and Warner, H. R. "The HELP System." *Journal of Medical Systems,* 1983, *7,* 87–102.

Reich, P. R., Geer, D. E., and Bleich, H. L. "A Computer Program for the Diagnosis of Hematological Disorders." *American Journal of Hematology,* 1977, *3,* 127–135.

Safran, C., Porter, D., Slack, W. V., and Bleich, H. L. "Diagnosis-Related Groups: A Critical Assessment of the Provision for Comorbidity." *Medical Care*, 1987, *25*, 1011–1014.

Safran, C., Slack, W. V., and Bleich, H. L. "Role of Computing in Patient Care in Two Hospitals." *M.D. Computing*, 1989, *6*(3), 141–148.

Scherrer, J. R., Baud, R. H., Hochstrasser, D., and Ratib, O. "An Integrated Hospital Information System in Geneva." *M.D. Computing*, 1990, *7*(2), 81–89.

Schwartz, W. B. "Medicine and the Computer: The Promise and Problems of Change." *New England Journal of Medicine*, 1970, *283*, 1257–1264.

Schwartz, W. B., Patil, R. S., and Szolovits, P. "Artificial Intelligence in Medicine: Where Do We Stand?" *New England Journal of Medicine*, 1987, *316*, 685–688.

Shortliffe, E. H., Davis, R., Axline, S. G., Buchanan, B. G., Green, C. C., and Cohen, S. N. "Computer-Based Consultations in Clinical Therapeutics: Explanation and Rule Acquisition Capabilities of the MYCIN System." *Computers and Biomedical Research*, 1975, *8*, 303–320.

Simborg, D. W., Chadwick, M., Whiting O'Keefe, Q. E., Tolchin, S. G., Kahn, S. A., and Bergan, E. S. "Local Area Networks and the Hospital." *Computers and Biomedical Research*, 1983, *16*, 247–259.

Slack, W. V. "The Computer and the Doctor-Patient Relationship." *M.D. Computing*, 1989, *6*(6), 320–321.

Slack, W. V. "How to Become a Genius." *M.D. Computing*, 1989, *6*(5), 262–263.

Slack, W. V., Safran, C., and Bleich, H. L. "Computerization in Hospital-Based Delivery Systems." In T. Trabin and M. A. Freeman (eds.), *The Computerization of Behavioral Healthcare: How to Enhance Clinical Practice, Management, and Communications.* San Francisco: Jossey-Bass, 1996.

Slack, W. V., and Slack, C. W. "Patient-Computer Dialogue." *New England Journal of Medicine*, 1972, *286*, 1304–1309.

Stead, W. W., and Hammond, W. E. "Computerized Medical Records: A New Resource for Clinical Decision Making." *Journal of Medical Systems*, 1983, *7*, 213–220.

Szolovits, P., Patil, R. S., and Schwartz, W. B. "Artificial Intelligence in Medical Diagnosis." *Annals of Internal Medicine*, 1988, *108*, 80–87.

Warner, H. R., Olmsted, C. M., and Rutherford, B. D. "HELP: A Program for Medical Decision-Making." *Computers and Biomedical Research*, 1972, *5*, 65–74.

Warner, H. R., Toronto, A. F., Veasey, L. G., and Stephenson, R. "A Mathematical Approach to Medical Diagnosis: Application to Congenital

Heart Disease." *Journal of the American Medical Association*, 1961, *177*(3), 177–183.

Weed, L. L. "Medical Records That Guide and Teach." *New England Journal of Medicine*, 1968, *278*, 593–600, 652–657.

Weed, L. L. "Technology Is a Link, Not a Barrier, for Doctor and Patient." *Modern Hospital*, 1970, *114*(2), 80–83.

Weizenbaum, J. *Computer Power and Human Reason*. New York: Freeman, 1976.

Whiting-O'Keefe, Q. E., Whiting, A., and Henke, J. "The STOR Clinical Information System." *M.D. Computing*, 1988, *5*, 8–21.

Chapter Seven

Barlam, T. F., Kowaloff, H. B., Zaleznik, D. F., Sands, K. E., and Slack, W. V. "Use of an Interactive Computer Program for Universal Precaution Training." Manuscript in preparation.

Bleich, H. L. "The Computer as a Consultant." *New England Journal of Medicine*, 1971, *284*, 141–147.

Bleich, H. L., Beckley, R. F., Horowitz, G., Jackson, J., Moody, E., Franklin, C., Goodman, S. R., McKay, M. W., Pope, R. A., Walden, T., Bloom, S. A., and Slack, W. V. "Clinical Computing in a Teaching Hospital." *New England Journal of Medicine*, 1985, *312*(12), 756–764.

Bleich, H. L., Safran, C., and Slack, W. V. "Departmental and Laboratory Computing in Two Hospitals." *M.D. Computing*, 1989, *6*, 149–155.

Bloom, S., White, R., Beckley, R., and Slack, W. "Converse: A Means to Write, Edit, Administer and Summarize Computer-Based Dialogue." *Computers and Biomedical Research*, 1978, *11*, 167–175.

Bourie, P., Chapman, R. H., Dai, S., and Reiley, P. "An Automated Nursing Assessment for a Teaching Hospital." *M.D. Computing*, 1997, *14*, 57–60.

Degoulet, P., Chatellier, G., Devries, V., Lavril, M., and Menard, J. "Computer-Assisted Techniques for Evaluation of Hypertensive Patients." *American Journal of Hypertension*, 1990, *3*, 156–163.

Einbinder, J. S., Rury, C., and Safran, C. "Outcomes Research Using the Electronic Patient Record: Beth Israel Hospital's Experience with Anticoagulation." In R. M. Gardner (ed.), *American Medical Informatics Association: The Proceedings of the Nineteenth Annual Symposium on Computer Applications in Medical Care*. Philadelphia: Hanley & Belfus, 1995.

Fordham, D., McPhee, S. J., Bird, J. A., Rodnick, J. E., and Detmer, W. M. "The Cancer Prevention Reminder System." *M.D. Computing*, 1990, *7*, 289–295.

Frame, P. S. "Can Computerized Reminder Systems Have an Impact on Preventive Services in Practice?" *Journal of General Internal Medicine (Supplement 5),* 1990, *5,* S112–S115.

Herrmann, F. R., Safran, C., Levkoff, S. E., and Minaker, K. L. "Serum Albumin Level on Admission as a Predictor of Death, Length of Stay, and Readmission." *Archives of Internal Medicine,* 1992, *152,* 125–130.

Horowitz, G. L., and Bleich, H. L. "PaperChase: A Computer Program to Search the Medical Literature." *New England Journal of Medicine,* 1981, *305,* 924–930.

Kuperman, G. J., Teich, J. M., Bates, D. W., Hiltz, F. L., Hurley, J. M., Lee, R. Y., and Paterno, M. D. "Detecting Alerts, Notifying the Physician, and Offering Action Items: A Comprehensive Alerting System." In J. J. Cimino (ed.), *A Symposium of the American Medical Informatics Association, October 26–30, 1996.* Philadelphia: Hanley & Belfus, 1995.

McCarty, R. J., Kanter, T., and Sopanen, J. *Lifeline.* Videotape documentary of clinical computing systems developed for Boston's Beth Israel and Brigham and Women's hospitals by the Center for Clinical Computing. Produced by RJM Associates, 1995.

McDonald, C. J. "Protocol-Based Computer Reminders, the Quality of Care and the Non-Perfectibility of Man." *New England Journal of Medicine,* 1976, *295*(24), 1351–1355.

McDonald, C. J., Wilson, G. A., and McCabe, G. P. "Physician Response to Computer Reminders." *Journal of the American Medical Association,* 1980, *244,* 1579–1581.

Mok, M. P., Castile, J. A., Kowaloff, H. B., and Janousek, J. R. "Drugman: A Computerized Supplement to a Hospital's Drug Information Newsletter." *American Journal of Hospital Pharmacy,* 1985, *42,* 1565–1567.

Ornstein, S. M., Garr, D. R., Jenkins, R. G., Rust, P. F., and Arnon, A. "Computer-Generated Physician and Patient Reminders: Tools to Improve Population Adherence to Selected Preventive Services." *Journal of Family Practice,* 1991, *32,* 82–90.

Pauker, S. G., Gorry, G. A., Kassirer, J. P., and Schwartz, W. B. "Towards the Simulation of Clinical Cognition: Taking a Present Illness by Computer." *American Journal of Medicine,* 1976, *60,* 981–996.

Pauker, S. G., and Kassirer, J. P. "Therapeutic Decision Making: A Cost-Benefit Analysis." *New England Journal of Medicine,* 1975, *293,* 229–234.

Physicians' Desk Reference. Montvale, N.J.: Medical Economics, 1996.

Rind, D. M., Safran, C., Phillips, R. S., Wang, Q., Calkins, D. R., Delbanco, T. L., Bleich, H. L., and Slack, W. V. "Effect of Computer-Based Alerts on the Treatment and Outcomes of Hospitalized Patients." *Archives of Internal Medicine*, 1994, *154*, 1511–1517.

Safran, C., Herrmann, F., Rind, D., Kowaloff, H., Bleich, H., and Slack, W. V. "Computer-Based Support for Clinical Decision Making." *M.D. Computing*, 1990, *7*(5), 319–322.

Safran, C., Porter, D., Lightfoot, J., Rury, C. D., Underhill, L. H., Bleich, H. L., and Slack, W. V. "ClinQuery: A System for Online Searching of Data in a Teaching Hospital." *Annals of Internal Medicine*, 1989, *9*, 751–756.

Safran, C., Rind, D. M., Davis, R. B., Ives, D., Sands, D. Z., Currier, J., Slack, W. V., Makadon, H. J., and Cotton, D. J. "Guidelines for Management of HIV Infection with Computer-Based Patient's Record." *Lancet*, 1995, *346*, 341–346.

Safran, C., Rury, C., Rind, D. M., and Taylor, W. C. "A Computer-Based Outpatient Medical Record for a Teaching Hospital." *M.D. Computing*, 1991, *8*(5), 291–299.

Safran, C., Slack, W. V., and Bleich, H. L. "Role of Computing in Patient Care in Two Hospitals." *M.D. Computing*, 1989, *6*(3), 141–148.

Sands, D. Z., and Safran, C. "Enhancing Patient Care with Computerized Clinical Formulas." *Clinical Research*, 1993, *41*, 527A.

Sands, D. Z., Safran, C., Slack, W. V., and Bleich, H. L. "Use of Electronic Mail in a Teaching Hospital." In *Seventeenth Annual Symposium on Computer Applications in Medical Care*. New York: McGraw-Hill, 1994.

Slack, W. V., Safran, C., and Bleich, H. L. "Computerization in Hospital-Based Delivery Systems." In T. Trabin and M. A. Freeman (eds.), *The Computerization of Behavioral Healthcare: How to Enhance Clinical Practice, Management, and Communications*. San Francisco: Jossey-Bass, 1996.

Tierney, W. M., McDonald, C. J., Martin, D. K., Hui, S. L., and Rogers, M. P. "Computerized Display of Past Test Results: Effect on Outpatient Testing." *Annals of Internal Medicine*, 1987, *107*, 569–574.

Warner, H. R., Olmsted, C. M., and Rutherford, B. D. "HELP: A Program for Medical Decision-Making." *Computers and Biomedical Research*, 1972, *5*, 65–74.

Weed, L. L. *Knowledge Coupling: New Premises and New Tools for Medical Care and Education*. New York: Springer-Verlag, 1991.

Wilson, G. A., McDonald, C. J., and McCabe, G. P., Jr. "The Effect of Immediate Access to a Computerized Medical Record on Physician Test

Ordering: A Controlled Clinical Trial in the Emergency Room." *American Journal of Public Health Care,* 1982, *72,* 698–702.

Chapter Eight

Bleich, H. L. "Medical Practice and Statistical Analysis." *M.D. Computing,* 1992, *9,* 281.

Bleich, H. L., Beckley, R. F., Horowitz, G., Jackson, J., Moody, E., Franklin, C., Goodman, S. R., McKay, M. W., Pope, R. A., Walden, T., Bloom, S. A., and Slack, W. V. "Clinical Computing in a Teaching Hospital." *New England Journal of Medicine,* 1985, *312*(12), 756–764.

Bleich, H. L., Safran, C., and Slack, W. V. "Departmental and Laboratory Computing in Two Hospitals." *M.D. Computing,* 1989, *6,* 149–155.

Bloom, S., White, R., Beckley, R., and Slack, W. "Converse: A Means to Write, Edit, Administer and Summarize Computer-Based Dialogue." *Computers and Biomedical Research,* 1978, *11,* 167–175.

Dewey, J. *Intelligence in the Modern World.* New York: Random House, 1939.

Feinstein, A. R. *Clinical Biostatistics.* Saint Louis: Mosby, 1977.

Glowniak, J. V., and Bushway, M. K. "Computer Networks as a Medical Resource: Accessing and Using the Internet." *Journal of the American Medical Association,* 1994, *271,* 1934–1939.

Goldberg, M. A. "Teleradiology and Telemedicine." *Radiology Clinics of North America,* 1996, *34*(3), 647–665.

Golden, P. A., Beauclair, R., and Sussman, L. "Factors Affecting Electronic Mail Use." *Computers in Human Behavior,* 1992, *8,* 297–311.

Hendrickson, G., Anderson, R. K., Clayton, P. D., Cimino, J., Hripcsak, G. M., Johnson, S. B., McCormack, M., Sengupta, S., Shea, S., Sideli, R., and Roderer, N. "The Integrated Academic Information Management System at Columbia-Presbyterian Medical Center." *M.D. Computing,* 1992, *9,* 35–42.

Hogarth, M. *An Internet Guide for the Health Professional.* Personal publication, mahogarth@ucdavis.edu, 1994.

Horowitz, G. L., and Bleich, H. L. "PaperChase: A Computer Program to Search the Medical Literature." *New England Journal of Medicine,* 1981, *305,* 924–930.

Horowitz, G. L., Jackson, J. D., and Bleich, H. L. "PaperChase: Self-Service Bibliographic Retrieval." *Journal of the American Medical Association,* 1983, *250*(18), 2494–2499.

Lindberg, D. A. "The National Library of Medicine and Its Role." *Bulletin of the Medical Library Association,* 1993, *81,* 71–73.

McConnell, J. "Medicine on the Superhighway." *Lancet,* 1993, *342,* 1313–1314.

McDonald, C. J., Wilson, G. A., McCabe, G. P. "Physician Response to Computer Reminders." *Journal of the American Medical Association,* 1980, *244,* 1579–1581.

McKinney, W. P., Wagner, J. M., Bunton, M. S., and Kirk, L. M. "A Guide to Mosaic and the World Wide Web for Physicians." *M.D. Computing,* 1995, *12*(2), 109–114, 141.

Nicoll, N. H. "Grateful Med: An Easy to Use Information Tool." *Reflections,* 1992, *18*(3), 40–41.

Pannen, M. "Guide to the Internet: The World Wide Web." *British Medical Journal,* 1995, *311,* 1552–1556.

Rind, D. M., Safran, C., Phillips, R. S., Wang, Q., Calkins, D. R., Delbanco, T. L., Bleich, H. L., and Slack, W. V. "Effect of Computer-Based Alerts on the Treatment and Outcomes of Hospitalized Patients." *Archives of Internal Medicine,* 1994, *154,* 1511–1517.

Safran, C., Herrmann, F., Rind, D., Kowaloff, H. B., Bleich, H. L., and Slack, W. V. "Computer-Based Support for Clinical Decision Making." *M.D. Computing,* 1990, *7*(5), 319–322.

Safran, C., Rind, D. M., Davis, R. B., Ives, D., Sands, D. Z., Currier, J., Slack, W. V., Makadon, H. J., and Cotton, D. J. "Guidelines for Management of HIV Infection with Computer-Based Patient's Record." *Lancet,* 1995, *346,* 341–346.

Safran, C., Slack, W. V., and Bleich, H. L. "Role of Computing in Patient Care in Two Hospitals." *M.D. Computing,* 1989, *6*(3), 141–148.

Sands, D. Z., Safran, C., Slack, W. V., and Bleich, H. L. "Use of Electronic Mail in a Teaching Hospital." In *Seventeenth Annual Symposium on Computer Applications in Medical Care.* New York: McGraw-Hill, 1994.

Slack, W. V. "Democracy and the Computer in America." *M.D. Computing,* 1992, *9*(6), 341–342.

Slack, W. V. "Assessing the Clinician's Use of Computers." *M.D. Computing,* 1993, *106,* 357–360.

Slack, W. V., Safran, C., and Bleich, H. L. "Computerization in Hospital-Based Delivery Systems." In T. Trabin and M. A. Freeman (eds.), *The Computerization of Behavioral Healthcare: How to Enhance Clinical Practice, Management, and Communications.* San Francisco: Jossey-Bass, 1996.

Slack, W. V., and Van Cura, L. J. "Patient Reaction to Computer-Based Medical Interviewing." *Computers and Biomedical Research,* 1968, *1,* 527–531.

Warner, H. R., Olmsted, C. M., and Rutherford, B. D. "HELP: A Program for Medical Decision-Making." *Computers and Biomedical Research*, 1972, *5*, 65–74.

Chapter Nine

Aronson, M.D. "Catch-22 in the Era of Peer Review Organizations." *M.D. Computing*, 1992, *9*, 284–285.

Barber, B. "Current Issues in Data Protection." *Medical Informatics (London)*, 1989, *14*, 207–209.

Barrows, R. C., Jr., and Clayton, P. D. "Privacy, Confidentiality, and Electronic Medical Records." *Journal of the American Medical Informatics Association*, 1996, *3*(2), 139–149.

Bleich, H. L. "Sidney R. Garfield and the Crisis in Health Care." *M.D. Computing*, 1994, *11*, 5–6.

Bleich, H. L., Beckley, R. F., Horowitz, G., Jackson, J., Moody, E., Franklin, C., Goodman, S. R., McKay, M. W., Pope, R. A., Walden, T., Bloom, S. A., and Slack, W. V. "Clinical Computing in a Teaching Hospital." *New England Journal of Medicine*, 1985, *312*(12), 756–764.

Bleich, H. L., Safran, C., and Slack, W. V. "Departmental and Laboratory Computing in Two Hospitals." *M.D. Computing*, 1989, *6*, 149–155.

Brannigan, V. M. "Patient Privacy: A Consumer Protection Approach." *Journal of Medical Systems*, 1984, *8*, 501–505.

Day, N. M. "Medical Information Bureau Report." *Transactions of the American Academy of Insurance Medicine Annual Meeting*, 1993, *76*, 18–20.

Entmacher, P. S. "Medical Information Bureau." *Journal of the American Medical Association*, 1975, *233*(13), 1370–1372.

Garfield, S. R. "The Delivery of Medical Care." *Scientific American*, 1970, *222*, 15–23.

Gritzalis, D., Katsikas, S., Keklikoglou, J., and Tomaras, A. "Data Security in Medical Information Systems: Technical Aspects of a Proposed Legislation." *Medical Informatics (London)*, 1991, *16*, 371–383.

Hiatt, H. H. *America's Health Care in the Balance: Choice or Chance*. New York: HarperCollins, 1987.

Kassirer, J. P. "Managed Care and the Morality of the Marketplace." *New England Journal of Medicine*, 1995, *333*, 50–52.

Robinson, E. N., Jr. "The Computerized Patient Record: Privacy and Security." *M.D. Computing*, 1994, *11*(2), 69–73.

Rosenberg, C. E. *The Care of Strangers: The Rise of America's Hospital System.* New York: Basic Books, 1987.

Rothfeder, J. *Privacy for Sale: How Computerization Has Made Everyone's Private Life an Open Secret.* New York: Simon & Schuster, 1992.

Safran, C., Porter, D., Lightfoot, J., Rury, C. D., Underhill, L. H., Bleich, H. L., and Slack, W. V. "ClinQuery: A System for Online Searching of Data in a Teaching Hospital." *Annals of Internal Medicine,* 1989, *9,* 751–756.

Safran, C., Rind, D., Citroen, M., Bakker, A. R., Slack, W. V., and Bleich, H. L. "Protection of Confidentiality in the Computer-Based Patient Record." *M.D. Computing,* 1995, *12*(3), 187–192.

Safran, C., Rury, C., Rind, D. M., and Taylor, W. C. "A Computer-Based Outpatient Medical Record for a Teaching Hospital." *M.D. Computing,* 1991, *8*(5), 291–299.

Safran, C., Slack, W. V., and Bleich, H. L. "Role of Computing in Patient Care in Two Hospitals." *M.D. Computing,* 1989, *6*(3), 141–148.

Shea, S. "Security Versus Access: Trade-Offs Are Only Part of the Story." *Journal of the American Medical Informatics Association,* 1994, *1,* 314–315.

Slack, W. V. "Patient Power." In J. A. Jacquez (ed.), *Computer Diagnosis and Diagnostic Methods: The Proceedings of the Second Conference on the Diagnostic Process Held at the University of Michigan.* Springfield, Ill.: Thomas, 1972.

Van der Leer, O. F. "The Use of Personal Data for Medical Research: How to Deal with New European Privacy Standards." *International Journal of Biomedical Computing,* 1994, *35* (Suppl.), 87–95.

Wald, J. S., Rind D, and Safran, C. "Protecting Confidentiality in an Electronic Medical Record: Feedback to the Author When Someone Reads a Clinical Note." *American Medical Informatics Association Spring Proceedings,* 1994.

Weed, L. L. "Medical Records That Guide and Teach." *New England Journal of Medicine,* 1968, *278,* 593–600, 652–657.

Weingarten, J. "Can Confidential Information Be Kept Private in High-Tech Medicine?" *M.D. Computing,* 1992, *9,* 79–82.

Chapter Ten

Bleich, H. L. "The Computer as a Consultant." *New England Journal of Medicine,* 1971, *284,* 141–147.

Bleich, H. L. "Charles Babbage and His Steam-Driven Computer." *M.D. Computing,* 1992, *9,* 6–10.

Brennan, P. F., Ripich, S., and Moore, S. M. "The Use of Home-Based Computers to Support Persons Living with AIDS/ARC." *Journal of Community Health Nursing,* 1991, *8*(1), 3–14.

Gustafson, D. H., Bosworth, K., Hawkins, R. P., Boberg, E. W., and Bricker, E. "CHESS: A Computer-Based System for Providing Information, Referrals, Decision Support and Social Support to People Facing Medical and Other Health-Related Crises." In M. E. Frisse (ed.), *Proceedings of the Sixteenth Annual Symposium on Computer Applications in Medical Care.* Baltimore: American Medical Informatics Association, 1992.

Gustafson, D. H., Hawkins, R. P., Boberg, E. W., Bricker, E., Pingree, S., and Chan, C. L. "The Use and Impact of a Computer-Based Support System for People Living with AIDS and HIV Infection." In J. G. Ozbolt (ed.), *Proceedings of the Eighteenth Annual Symposium on Computer Applications in Medical Care.* Washington, D.C.: American Medical Informatics Association, 1994.

McTavish, F. M., Gustafson, D. H., Owens, B. H., Hawkins, R. P., Pingree, S., Wise, M., Taylor, J. O., and Apantaku, F. M. "CHESS (Comprehensive Health Enhancement Support System), an Interactive Computer System for Women with Breast Cancer Piloted with an Underserved Population." *Journal of Ambulatory Care Management,* 1995, *18*(3), 35–41.

Parkinson, C. N. *Parkinson's Law.* New York: Ballantine, 1987.

Skinner, B. F. *The Behavior of Organisms: An Experimental Analysis.* Englewood Cliffs, N.J.: Appleton-Century-Crofts, 1938.

Slack, W. V. "Use of Computers." In *MEDINFO 80, Proceedings of the Third World Conference on Medical Informatics.* Amsterdam: North Holland, 1980.

Slack, W. V. "The Soul of a New System: a Modern Parable." *Massachusetts Medicine,* 1987, *2,* 24–28.

Slack, W. V. "A Brief Treatise on the Academic Committee." *M.D. Computing,* 1990, *7*(5), 282–284.

Slack, W. V. "Type 1 and Type 2 Administrators." *M.D. Computing,* 1990, *7*(2), 69–70.

Slack, W. V. "The Forces of Bureaucracy." *M.D. Computing,* 1992, *9*(3), 133–135.

Slack, W. V. "When the Machine Stops." *M.D. Computing,* 1992, *9*(1), 6–10.

Slack, W. V., Boro, E. S., and Bleich, H. L. "Barriers to Clinical Computing: What Physicians Can Do." *M.D. Computing,* 1992, *9,* 278–280.

Slack, W. V., Van Cura, L. J., and Greist, J. H. "Computers and Doctors: Use and Consequences." *Computers and Biomedical Research,* 1970, *3,* 521–527.

Von Neumann, J. *The Computer and the Brain.* New Haven, Conn.: Yale University Press, 1958.

Watson, J. B. *Behaviorism.* New York: Norton, 1924.

Woolhandler, S., Himmelstein, D. U., and Lewontin, J. P. "Administrative Costs in U.S. Hospitals." *New England Journal of Medicine,* 1993, *329,* 400–403.

Chapter Eleven

Feinstein, A. R. "Twentieth Century Paradigms That Threaten Both Scientific and Humane Medicine in the Twenty-First Century." *Journal of Clinical Epidemiology,* 1996, *49,* 615–617.

Hiatt, H. H. *America's Health Care in the Balance: Choice or Chance.* New York: HarperCollins, 1987.

Miller, R. A., Schaffner, K. F., and Meisel, A. "Ethical and Legal Issues Related to the Use of Computer Programs in Clinical Medicine." *Annals of Internal Medicine,* 1985, *102,* 529–537.

Slack, W. V., Boro, E. S., and Bleich, H. L. "Barriers to Clinical Computing: What Physicians Can Do." *M.D. Computing,* 1992, *9,* 278–280.

Epilogue

de Tocqueville, A. *Democracy in America.* (G. Lawrence, trans.). Garden City, N.Y.: Doubleday, 1969.

Forster, E. M. "The Machine Stops." In *The Eternal Moment and Other Stories.* Orlando: Harcourt Brace, 1928.

Slack, W. V. "When the Machine Stops." *M.D. Computing,* 1992, *9*(1), 6–10.

Slack, W. V. "When the Home Is Also the Clinic." *M.D. Computing,* 1996, *13*(6), 465–468.

—— About the Author

WARNER V. SLACK received his bachelor's degree from Princeton University, his medical degree from Columbia University's College of Physicians and Surgeons, and his residency training in neurology at the University of Wisconsin. His early work in computer-based medical interviewing at the University of Wisconsin led to the development of the first computer-based medical history. Over the past thirty years he has done extensive research in the field of patient-computer dialogue. He has developed and studied programs that provide direct assistance to the patient in the management of common, important medical and psychological problems. He was an early advocate of the patient's right to participate in decisions about diagnosis and treatment.

During the past twenty years, Dr. Slack and his colleagues at the Center for Clinical Computing (CCC) and the Harvard Medical School have developed, implemented, and evaluated an integrated, hospital-wide clinical computing system (the CCC system) that is used in patient care at Beth Israel Hospital and Brigham and Women's Hospital in Boston.

Pursuing his interest in the field of mental testing, Dr. Slack has also examined the use and misuse of the Scholastic Aptitude Test. The results from his studies, done in collaboration with Dr. Douglas Porter, have been influential in reformative efforts, such as the "truth in testing" legislation passed in New York State.

Dr. Slack is co-president, with Dr. Howard Bleich, of the Center for Clinical Computing. He is also associate professor of medicine and psychiatry at Harvard Medical School, and the editor in chief of *M.D. Computing*.

⁓ Index